Blessings

xx
Jeanne

The Goddess You

principles for living in soul alignment

By Jeanne Street

Illustrated By Kari Del Vecchio

INSPIRIT

HEAL   LEARN   GROW

By Design

New Milford CT

The Goddess You   principles for living in soul alignment
By Jeanne Street

Published by: Inspirit by Design, a division of Jeanne Street LLC, New Milford, Connecticut
Cover & interior design and illustrations by: Kari Del Vecchio of Kari D. Designs. Bridgewater, Connecticut

Library of Congress Control Cataloging in Publication Data available on file.

ISBN:978-0-9974666-1-4

First Edition, November 2016
Printed in the United States Of America

Dedicated To my Angels

for gently guiding me through the

darkness and forward into the light,

reminding me of God's unending love.

Contents

Introduction   9

The Twelve Principles

One   Quieting the Mind   29

Two   Self-Love   39

Three   Changing Your Reactions   51

Four   Energy Basics   61

Five   Healing the Block   77

Six   Let It Go   87

Seven   Chakra Basics   95

Eight   Healthy, Wealthy and Wise   107

Nine   Keep Calm   121

Ten   Help, I've Lost My Balance   131

Eleven   Mind, Body and Spirit   141

Twelve   Intuitive, Gifted You   151

The Goddess You
principles for
living in soul alignment

Introduction

This lovely book you hold in your hands right now is about leaving no stone unturned in your life. Or perhaps more than that, having no part of your life that Divine love does not heal.

That is my invitation to you. With that in mind, let me give you a window into why I called this book The Goddess You *principles for living in soul alignment*.

You are the Goddess You.

This one thought opens up a whole new pathway, one that leads to principles, or fundamental truths, in which you can live a more abundant, joy-filled, happy, soul-aligned life.

Soul alignment is the destination. I define it as that state of being when your soul is in alignment with God's energy. Your soul is and always has been connected to Divine love, source of all. Each and every person has God-spark light within them. Your journey in this life has lessons, challenges and experiences that can distance you from the truth, which is that you are and always have been a child of God. Soul alignment leads to your knowing and understanding the who, what, why and where about you and your life's purpose. The origin point is knowing your true self, the Goddess You Self. But at some point, we fall out of true soul alignment.

I call this the addiction to not being you. It is indeed an addiction. Trust me when I tell you that I personally know of this addiction all too well. You fuel your addiction to not being you with self-doubt and loathing. You feed it negativity and fear. You choose to hide behind the walls of stories, pain, suffering or life events. The blame-shame game seems to take over your thoughts. Drama feeds off the energy because you keep serving it up. It's like a hellish roller coaster ride, and you just can't seem to get off.

You know something is missing in your life. You notice these thoughts, the pain, the blame, the shame and the drama. And that leads you to contemplating these thoughts, and questioning them—the five Ws: the who, what, where, when and why. This knowing is your intuition, and it's the path to your soul-aligned life.

Every person has this inner guidance system known as intuition. When you connect your intuition to God source, it is called alignment. When you are aligned to your Soul Self, you can learn to utilize your intuition in a heightened way because grooving in soul alignment allows for your intuition to guide and lead you in a Divine direction.

You have probably already been using this inner guidance system. It brought you to this book. Questioning the who, what, where, when and why of your life brought you to a new mindset—and now, a new willingness. Perhaps it is more than willingness. Perhaps now you crave for change.

Heed that craving. That craving is what helps you admit that you are not living fully in your soul alignment. Thus begins your search—the search to find who you are, why you are here, what your gifts and talents are and where to find the balance you seek. The "when" comes at the moment you say, "Yes, I am ready."

Maybe your search began with books, classes, or even talk therapy. Maybe you felt lost within your life, depleted and out of sorts. Now you can look back and realize you are not the person you once dreamed of being. There are some moments that resemble that person— you know, the real you - who once was present in her own life. Or, maybe you are like so many others who have *never* really known their authentic Goddess self.

That is not who you are! I know this, you know this, but somehow your life does not seem to resemble this. Why? Who is the Goddess within you, and is she within your reach?

The Goddess You, is indeed you. You, my friend, are perfection in every single way. You've just lost the view, and your connection to your groovy Goddess self. Life has taken you on a joy ride of ups and downs and ins and outs. Life has provided lessons to be lived and learned. Sometimes they have been on replay until you find the truth they offer. Obstacles have slowed you down or even sometimes stopped you. This is truth for every human soul. You are here within your life to learn, grow and remember your God connection.

Life's challenges can become so big that you forget to see the light of joy within your very own reflection. Once that light dims, you can no longer see the light in others clearly. This is when judgments, resentments, anger and fear creep in—ever so slightly, and seemingly without your permission. Add in family, jobs, divorce, illness, carpooling, kids or any other of your life's busyness to complicate and block the joy. Trudging through your daily routine seems so exhausting that anxiety finds a way in. Troubled relationships lead to a drama vortex. Mini tornadoes of over-reactivity—occupy the place where joy once lived. Your mind spins from the buzz of the crazy, and the lack of joy leaves you lonely, sad and isolated.

Yup, this can sound super depressing when you can identify yourself in a book written by someone you may not personally know and recognize your life between the lines. On the flip side it is oftentimes a godsend that a book can actually relate to you—I mean really relate—on a soul level. Another human soul can really see and understand your pain and write about it.

What if . . . this person you don't know personally but who can understand your pain can help you to heal and live in your soul alignment? What would your life look like then? Would you be happy in this new found soul alignment? Would you know who you actually are? Would your work

then be fulfilling? Would your family be supportive? Would your willingness to shift your life be strong enough to get you to your goal? Ask yourself: When can this alignment happen for me?

Let me interject here for a moment with how I see it from my point of view: I can see that yes, you can do this. And of course, if you don't already know, the truth is that yes, indeed, your pain can aid in your growth and in discovering your life's purpose. This truth will fill you with profound joy. Your work will shift and be in alignment with your amazing Soul Self. Your family will support and love you when you make shifts that line up with the real you. You are more powerful than you ever imagined. Your strength will see you through, and love will patiently wait, no matter how long it takes. Living in soul alignment is not a race or show of skills, but rather a way of life; so when you are ready, you can align. You may be wondering how I can be so sure of this. Well, come along with me, and you shall see. And by the way, I'm so glad you are here.

Getting to Know Me

So, here is my cue-in. I am Jeanne Street, and I am a spiritual medium. I've been guided to pass along the Goddess You principles, so that you and others with similar addictions of not living in soul alignment may find peace, love and joy. My gift allows me to connect with others on a soul level. I have the gift of seeing, feeling and knowing just what someone should do to heal pains, resolve life events and live with joy and love. This is my "why" for sharing the Goddess principles with you.

Through the gift of mediumship, I have channeled the healing Goddess You principles within this book and its companion *The Goddess You Journal*. The companion journal provides a place for you to explore the principles, with writing prompts specific to deepening the practice of each principle. Spirit shared these life-changing principles that are Divine in nature and meant for your healing. Through each of the principles, you will find the layering of clarity on your personal discovery of your soul identity.

I have learned from Divine connection, witnessing firsthand with clients and in my personal life that healing comes in layers. Although you may feel you have already moved past something and have let go of it or feel you don't wish to open an old wound, Spirit taught me that healing is similar to layers of an onion. Each layer has a unique quality to it. The quality can bring forth tears or other uncomfortable feelings. These feelings are key in your healing. Burying the layers of your onion within creates sourness in life. With the gentle guidance of Spirit's love and support contained in the principles, you can learn to move through these layers with ease.

In the chapters ahead, you will embark on a journey like no other. I will offer you a view into my personal healing journey and some of my clients' healing journeys as a guide for you to witness the principles at work. Know that as you walk forward, you are supported by another who has followed the principles and continues to live them every day. Rest assure, that soul alignment is within your reach. As you begin to groove in your Goddess alignment, your intuition will spark a newfound connection. Your life will shift, joy will make a comeback, and love will lead you to your soul's answers and alignment.

Angels, Guides & Spirit, Oh My!

Before I take you too much further into this new way of being with Spirit, I need to explain a few examples of how I use my words. So, just who is this Spirit that I write about?

Tone. The Oxford English Dictionary defines tone as a modulation of the voice that may express a particular feeling or mood. But for me, the word encompasses so much more. A tone is a sound or quality in which someone, something or some situation speaks through any one of my senses.

For instance, in a recent client reading/healing session, it became clear she had a tumor. The tumor itself spoke to me in a tone. It came first as a knowing, then it came through in the sense of taste. The taste was metallic. Then it spoke to me of being dull and flat. Next came a feeling, which spoke to the tumor being solid matter. After that, it entered my sense of sight: it revealed itself and I could see the tumor in all the layers as a certain shape.

The Angels speak to me in a tone of truth. They can seem matter-of-fact in tone, without a lot of emotion, but a better way to describe it is to say they speak with the purity of love.

Vibration. Merriam-Webster defines vibration as an instance of vibrating, but more informally, as a person's emotional state. Spirit speaks to me in the vibration of energy. The vibrational rate reveals the wellbeing of the person, thing, or situation I am working with. In the case of my client with the tumor, her vibrational rate was low and heavy which revealed depletion in several areas of her body. The tone and vibrational rate was metallic, which led to my understanding that the tumor's source was metal toxicity.

Energy. The ordinary dictionary definition of energy is the strength and vitality required for sustained physical or mental activity. But my definition starts with the idea that everything is made up of energy; therefore energy can be felt through all of the senses. Energy readings allow me to know the well-being of the person or situation. I often receive the energy information through color, which is how auras can be seen and read. My client with the tumor was definitely emitting the energy of depletion, revealing that the tumor was robbing her of nutrients. The combination of the tone, vibration and energy of the tumor brought the whole tumor into focus.

In breaking all of this down, you can see that readings are done in levels. Sometimes the message comes in visuals, through signs and symbols that take shape and reveal a deeper connection to the senses. Or the messages are received through complex layers of tone, vibration and energy.

Often when I am connecting with someone's loved one who has crossed over, the information comes in stages. By training myself to tune into Spirit's voice, I have developed a way to move through the stages quickly. The average person would likely not notice the information that is filtering through me. To listen to Spirit's voice, a medium must connect each sense to the individual person or situation. Once the connection is made, the medium can process each layer fairly quickly.

The energy of spiritual beings is clean, pure and all love. Even our loved ones who have crossed over have been cleansed to purify their tone, vibration and energy.

Spirit. This is how I refer to any and all connections from the spiritual realm. This includes Guides, Angels, Archangels, Ascended Masters or loved ones who have crossed over. Basically, Spirit is all the beings that God's energy encompasses!

Guides. This is how I refer to my team, or yours, on the other side. Each and every one of us has at least one guide who is there to gently support us. Your guides can change as you grow into new areas of your life. And while a family

15

member can be a guide, it is not likely to be someone you will have met in this lifetime. Although our loved ones can visit us and send supportive loving messages, they have work to do on the other side to reflect and learn from their life here on earth.

Angels. Angels are God's love poured into these Divine beings.

Archangels. Archangels work directly with God as his Divine team. Calling upon the Archangels in prayer will super size your prayer!

Here a few Archangels whom you can call upon to assist you.

Archangel Michael is known as the protector of God. Call on Michael when you need courage or protection.

Archangel Gabriel is known as the messenger of God. Call on Gabriel for assistance in clear speaking.

Archangel Raphael is known as the healer. Call on Raphael when you or a loved one is ill.

Archangel Uriel is known as the light of God. Call on Uriel for clear insight.

Guardian Angels. We are assigned at least one Guardian Angel who stays with us for life. Our Guardian Angels can guide us when we are open to receiving their loving help. While Angels can help guide and assist us in need, they cannot interfere with free will. Calling upon your Angels will give them permission to lend a wing in time of need.

Empath. An empath is a person who can literally experience the feelings, emotions and illnesses of others.

Clairs. The "clair" sisters are the way we receive messages from the spirit realm. I will explain some of the different clairs more in depth in the chapters ahead, but for now, know that they include ways of seeing, sensing, hearing, tasting, speaking and knowing.

- Clairvoyance
- Clairsentience
- Clairaudience
- Clairalience
- Clairgustance

- Clairenunuciate

- Claircogniance

Knowing. Psychic insight combined with any one or more of the clairs. Knowing allows Spirit to connect you to the flow of the messages and channels them through your senses.

Psychic. A psychic is a person who can pick up psychic impressions of another person's energy. (Note: Psychics are not mediums.)

Medium. A medium is a person who can connect to Spirit through one or more of the clairs. (Note: All mediums are psychic.)

Through the spiritual guidance of the twelve Goddess principles, I found my gifts began to open and restore their balance. My God-spark—you know the God-spark that lives within each and every one of us—began to shine brightly once again without flickering. My faith deepened, relationships healed and old friends left way for new higher vibrational ones to come in and take their place. So many shifts in my life happened when I took the plunge and let faith lead the way instead of fear.

Your path will also be shifting and changing as you implement each of the twelve principles into your life. Your journal will play an important role. Subtle shifts may be present at first, but the magic will happen when you can reflect back on those first journal entries. You will see with the clarity, heightened intuition, knowing and insight that have come to you from actively practicing the twelve principles.

So, grab your *Goddess You Journal* now and write your first entry:

Tell how you imagine your life will look after you start following the principles.

What I have come to fully trust in and see is that Spirit's love is endless for every living being.

My prayer for you is that you, too, find the comfort and truth in your Goddess Soul Self. That the fear dissipates before your eyes and love fills the void in your life. May the love of God fill you, bless you, and keep you in his unending mercy.

Blessings,

XX Jeanne

The Addiction of Not Being Me

Spirit's voice became part of my everyday reality in 2007. Just as quickly as it had shut down when I was a child, it returned years later when I was an adult. I had spent years ignoring Spirit's voice, hiding behind a person I no longer recognized as me. Drama, gossip, overindulgence—those were some of the energies that kept my true identity a secret, one that even I needed help uncovering to see. Now, I was being reborn. My path back was one of enlightenment and spiritual attunement.

One day I woke up, saw how unfulfilled I was—lost and so far out of touch with my sense of self that I almost did not recognize my own reflection or hear my own voice. As I look back on this moment, I understand that what I was actually seeing in my reflection was what I refer to now as wearing an "Edgar suit," referencing that scene from Men in Black when an alien takes over a character's body. His face is recognizable, but his soul doesn't seem to be present in his body. That's what I looked like. I couldn't see my soul or God-spark light. I was not living in soul alignment.

Later on, Spirit continued to show me the sign of the "Edgar suit" as I started to work with clients. Spirit impressed upon me how to recognize when a person's soul is not fully connected or aligned to the Soul Self: your soul doesn't fill out your body with the light or energy of Spirit. These revelations called on me to reflect back on my life, in which I had worked hard at many different jobs that had nothing to do with fulfilling my soul's work, just to satisfy the fear-based thinking to which I once was drawn and in which I had been very stuck.

Fear, a.k.a. my ego, kept me hostage within my own life, a very private, confined cell in which I stayed for a long time. I had practiced daily doses of self-sabotage, deflating my sense of self-worth. What was I fearful of—the truth? Why would ego not want me to know? Who was I really?

Do you recognize some of this tone in your life? This is a perfect opportunity to grab your **Goddess You Journal** and tell me about your Edgar suit.

What I came to know was that ego had twisted my view on life, keeping me in the shadow of reality. I had become compliant to fear and lost my connection to my Soul Self. It was not one main event that happened to me—not one cause, not a single catalyst—that woke me up, but rather fear that had accumulated to such a point that I finally could see. During that wake-up period, I came to see how fear had attached itself to me. I started noticing how many ways fear had become a way of life, separating me from my soul connection.

Every day, it was becoming clearer that my life had become unrecognizable and was no longer aligned with my soul truth. I was not doing the work that filled me with joy and passion. I was stuck in stories of the past. I held onto the lack of self-worth. The past affected my present. I was lost within my own life. I denied my truths to cover up my pain and to avoid hurting others. Yet, as a result, I caused more pain to myself. By not speaking about and releasing the events of the past, I gave them power over me. These are the "things" that caused the disconnection from my Soul Self.

Thus it was that in early 2007, I fully embraced the whisper of Spirit, awakening my well-kept secret. Although I had heard these whispers before, I had grown accustomed to ignoring or shooing them away as if they were nothing more than my imagination. Once I decided to listen to the whisper from Spirit, one message led to another, then another.

Although I was stubborn and unsure, Spirit kept nudging, until I finally allowed myself to "see" once again. Spirit was guiding me with love and kindness, and the tone was that I had much work to do to recover from the addiction of not being me. Yes, the false sense of who I was turned out to be an addiction to fear— until Spirit pointed out that my ego was fueling the fear addiction and I would stay in the same energy unless I got to work and followed the Divine guidance! Spirit showed me that within the principles of the Goddess You, what I lacked was self-love. To raise my energetic vibration, I would have to change my world view, and fast! Tough love had a whole new meaning to me now.

What Spirit also taught me was that I was an empath and that living and being an empath requires one's full attention. Remember, an empath is someone who experiences the feelings of others in a physiological way. This tone was loud and clear from Spirit. I had to clean up my energy to allow for my inner light to shine and do the work my soul had been attuned to do. I will be honest with you: this was not an easy journey for me to embark on but one that was so worth every tear along the way. You will find this true for your journey as well. Remember healing happens in onion layers, sometimes you get a layer that downright takes your breath away. You simply push through the task of peeling your onion, wiping the tears away and cherishing the moment you are done!

Divine Intervention

I owned a shoe boutique, and one ordinary day, while I was unpacking a new shipment of beautiful shoes, a man walked into my shop. To set the scene: Sassy Shoe was on a main thruway with lots of traffic. My building had two storefronts, one of which was empty.

As this man entered, I immediately heard Spirit's tone along with my knowing kick in. I felt this crazy, strong gut feeling to get behind the checkout area. Picture the room: I had purchased an old bar at a tag sale, which I'd refinished in an antiqued, rustic style. The bar served as the boutique's checkout area. It was kitty-corner in the back of the boutique's front room. I quickly moved behind the bar and took out some paperwork to look busy while I also rifled around for the phone and a makeshift weapon (a pair of scissors) to hold near. All the while, I engaged in conversation with this man about what or whom he was shopping for—a wife or girlfriend—I was seeing the color red in my mind. I knew it was Spirit's messages and that I just had to keep calm. I asked if he was looking for a gift; he spoke in a tone that came to me as soft and scary. I "knew" in that instance he was there to hurt me; the red in my view got brighter and closer. Spirit's voice told me to stay behind the bar, be calm and wait for the phone to ring. I said a prayer and thought of my hubby, and just then the phone rang! As I picked up the phone, Spirit led me to break the energetic eye contact and instructed me to not look at him directly which would allow the negative energy of that moment to be broken. As I did this, the man moved away from the shoe rack and made his way to the door and left. Spirits voice then led me to the window to note the make, model and plate number of his car as I watched his vehicle leave. I grabbed my car keys, locked the front door and left a few minutes later to pick up my youngest daughter at school.

As I drove, I felt a calm come over me. When we returned to the shop from her school, I noticed I felt safe. As new customers came in, the energy returned to a normal flow, and I was able to put the incident aside—that is, for the time being.

It is important to note this as a miraculous moment for me as I was easily able to let go of the drama and fear that normally would have consumed me.

The next morning, I woke with the same voice speaking to me, "He will return." I felt uneasy, and my knowing confirmed Spirit's message. I immediately called my husband and told him the events of the previous day, how I had seen the color red and heard a voice that spoke to me. I also told him that I could not go to work that day or to the space again. He agreed. I knew if I returned to that space that man would be back to hurt me. I set my mind and intention to find a new location to lease.

I drove to our picturesque New England down-town, and low and behold there was a vacant shop with an amazing store front window. It was perfect timing. I called the number advertised on the door, met with the owner, signed the lease and had my shop moved to the new location within three days. Because I decided in that moment to trust what Spirit was showing me I felt divinely supported and magically everything fell into place. My parents helped me paint the new space. My husband and sons moved all of the furniture, while my daughters and I moved the merchandise.

Thank God for family and for the angelic guidance that led me to this lovely new space. The new location was surrounded by all types of shops, restaurants, salons and boutiques, and had a constant flow of people working, eating, shopping and just strolling by. Divine intervention at its best!

Awakening

As time went on, I began uniting with my soul on a healing journey, with Spirit's guidance leading me to the Goddess You principles. Spirit began putting amazing people in my path, people who would open my view to the world of metaphysical studies. As I began growing and learning more in alignment with my Soul Self, my life began to take major shifts. I was shown signs of closing my shop. Writing came back into my view. Purging old ways opened the pathway for change. I began to understand that the "knowing" I experienced was my gift, and that being an empath required my full attention. Meditation and prayer became part of my every day routine. My journey led me to close my shoe boutique and step onto a new pathway of healing. I entered a brand new phase in life, honoring and embracing my gifts, healing from past events and moving away from toxic relationships. Forgiveness came in and taught me how forgiving myself and others could and would set me free of the pain and suffering that I had internalized. Forgiveness also let love and compassion in to open my heart while inviting healing into many aspects of my life.

Goddess You Journal

The question I am asked all the time is, "Where do I start?"

First, and foremost, you start with a journal. Your journal will be your best friend over the next twelve weeks. You will use your journal every day, throughout the day.

You may choose to work with *The Goddess You Journal*, which I wrote to accompany this book. It adds depth to your journey by bringing each principle into your life with the addition of guided writing prompts that provide a focus on the principle at hand, leading you closer to your soul alignment. You can find out more about *The Goddess You Journal* by visiting my website www.jeannestreet.com. You may also choose to purchase a journal on your own and write about whatever you want! If you choose the later, it doesn't have to be fancy, a simple notebook will do the trick.

Journaling has been proven scientifically to remove mental blocks. This is done by keeping your pen in contact with paper. Allowing the analytical left brain to keep focus on the writing while the creative right side can flow. This allows you to connect with true feelings and work through blocks.

Journaling

- **Reduces stress and anxiety**

- **Aligns you to your truth**

- **Helps you to move through troubled areas of your life**

- **Helps you heal from past events**

Before you begin your journey, you will need the following:

1. a journal and dedicated pen (It's important to keep a pen with your journal!)

2. a notebook for your homework

3. thirty minutes a day devoted to yourself

And that is all you need to start! Sounds pretty easy, doesn't it? Give yourself thirty minutes of "you" time. I know we are all busy, but trust me, when you learn to add this time into your day, you are creating a sacred contract with your Inner Goddess. You are allowing her the ability to work in harmony with you. You will feel the difference right away.

Onward and upward you go!

Discovering your Goddess Purpose

So, if you're like I was, living a life that is not recognizable to you, maybe you are wondering what's a girl to do when nothing seems to make sense about you anymore? Who you once were is now hidden behind a career, children or a life created out of fear of following your passion. You may even question, like I once did: What is the passion for which I am longing? Can I not remember how to find it? You may also be wondering: What is my purpose here within this family, in this life, in this job? Perhaps you yearn for more fulfilling days and nights. This book and **The Goddess You Journal** can be your guides so you can find clarity and alignment while implementing the Goddess You principles into your life.

It will lead you on your personal discovery to uncovering your soul identity. How, you may wonder, do I know this for sure? Well, because as you will see in the chapters ahead, I was stuck in the smallness of who I thought I was. With the loving guidance of Spirit, I shed the old and began living the life I had dreamed that I could have. I am proof that anyone who has the wish to shift and change her life can do so.

The truth is, the desired outcome is within your very reach.

The Goddess You principles that Spirit so lovingly shared with me - the life changing principles- are gifts of Divine love meant to heal those in need. Journaling can help you achieve living your inner truth while healing your pains, blocks, suffering or any life event that keeps you stuck inside a life that is unfulfilling. It is my recommendation that you devote at least one week for each of the twelve principles and that you journal your way through each chapter and its corresponding lesson. The weekly pace will help you gain insight and strengthen your intuitive voice.

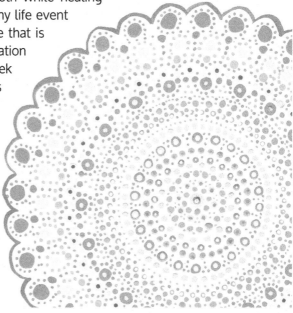

Bonus Factor

Your **Goddess You Journal** can also be the medium in which Spirit's voice speaks to you. This technique is called automatic writing. Automatic writing is when you allow Spirit to move through you in an energetic way. The pen is the connection, and the paper is the receiving point for the message.

Spirit has shown and taught me that although you may feel you have healed a layer of the pain, suffering or block, endless layers continue to need healing, which also allows your soul to grow in the lessons and lifework you are here to accomplish. That is why the Goddess You principles can be used time and time again to work through different levels of your healing journey. Each time you put the principles into practice, your life will shift and transform into a more fulfilling easy-to-embrace state of being.

Principle One

Quieting the Mind

As I opened up, Spirit began to help me out of the funk of my life. The message that kept coming, was that to begin to open my gift fully, I would have to learn to stop the chatter in my head that was there twenty-four hours a day, seven days a week. This was no easy task. Even getting the message to quiet my mind took a long time to fully receive. As I said, I had been asleep in my life and from my gifts from a young age. So the Angels had their work cut out for them.

Spirit began with nudges—that is how I can best describe the tones I first began to receive. (Remember, tones are more than voice; they are the quality through which someone, something or a situation speaks through one of our senses.) Nudges to meditate, nudges to not gossip, nudges to listen instead of speaking—all came to me. Sometimes I listened to the nudge, and other times I ignored it. What I began to notice after some time was that when I ignored the nudge, I would get a heightened sensation around my head, then goose bumps on the back of my neck. I could not shake off the goose bump sensation easily. This led me to pay attention to the nudges. I started to question where they were coming from.

I had previously learned about guides and Angels in books I had read and began asking in my thoughts if the nudges were Spirit speaking. I began to feel their presence through this heightened feeling and through these nudges.

Of course I had my doubts that I was actually connecting to the Spirit realm. My fear or ego thoughts I had been living with for so long kept tugging at me, trying to keep me from believing this was truly Spirit. My faith, with my willingness to see the confirmations from my spiritual team, slowly began the reversal of those thoughts.

Quiet the mind messages came in many ways from my spiritual team: from books to radio messages, and conversations with others, they started to get louder and louder. Ironically my inner radio volume needed adjusting so I could hear the tone of Spirit over my mind chatter.

Spirit led me to meditation and breath work so I could begin this journey of quieting my mind. Stopping the constant chatter was going to take a lot of time. I realized I was participating in all of the mini-drama sessions carried on in my thoughts, daily to-do lists, what was for dinner, what plans we had for the holidays and on and on and on. I was shown that I was wearing my energy out with these constant thoughts. I was led to journal some of these stories. This was not at all easy for me because I judged my tone and voice. As I began releasing the stories on paper, a shift in the tone of the stories started to occur. I began to see the volume along with the energetic lower vibration these stories had. They were like beach balls filled with sand and a radio blasting in the center of each ball. These balls, or stories, were weighing me down.

Spirit guided me to incorporate a daily practice of breath connection. I was struggling during this time with meditating and being present. Learning to stay with my breath from start to finish helped me to let go and be one with my body. This worked like a charm, so I began to practice the breath connection during the day whenever I noticed my mind slipping off into the thought abyss. This breath connection was my new best friend. We began hanging out in blissful quiet more and more. All this quiet time allowed Spirit room for sending me more messages.

Spirit began to show me the importance of knowing and understanding fear, the voice of ego. I was guided to hear the negative tone of ego and the love tone of Spirit. I was really taken back how my fearful mind and ego-voice had manipulated my daily thoughts and my life, along with the reality that I had allowed this to take place.

As you may imagine, I experienced many emotions that I had to work through from my years of ego thought and living in fear. The fact that I let this tone take up so much of my life was a bit depressing. Spirit offered support for the lull in my mood by reminding me of God's unending love and how the miracle of self-love invites the return to original love.

Soon enough, with Spirit's loving support, I learned the difference in the tones of love and ego. "Shmego," as I refer to him now, is the tricky little bastard that lives in your head and whose only goal is to keep you living a fear-based life.

Spirit taught me that this Shmego guy was the one thing that kept me from living in full alignment with God and original love.

Spirit's lesson showed me that thoughts become energy. The energy of the thought becomes the life you lead. Thus your thoughts become your reality. Let me say that again for you: **your thoughts become your reality.**

Although I grew up knowing God and was raised in the Catholic faith, I did not really feel as close to God as I once had in my childhood. I missed God and wanted wholeheartedly to restore our relationship.

Somewhere along the way I had forgotten how to be in God's love. Not only had I forgotten how to be in God's love, but that stupid Shmego guy also kept me from embracing my faith fully. Fear of being a sinner and out of the reach of God's love, fear of not understanding and knowing the Catholic faith fully, fear of others being holier than me—these thoughts and others were the yucky layers I had built into the self-loathing system in which I had been living.

Spirit's guidance led me to the understanding that we are all connected to the Divine. God's light lives within each and every living being. Religion is human-made and serves as a beautiful place to worship with like-minded people. But no four walls can hold God's energy. He is everywhere and is everything. God is called many different names. I was shown that my faith in God would heal the fearful thinking that kept me from feeling his presence.

Confirmation

One Sunday I witnessed Angels on the altar during mass. As the priest was preparing the Eucharist, Spirit's energy came before me as the Angels gathered around the altar. This lovely holy view was followed with a loving message that with every celebration of God, the Angels come rejoicing his holy name, no matter what religion you choose. This was powerful for me.

And so I pondered it again: no four walls can contain God. Hmmm, this made perfect sense to me on a soul level. I understood that religion is unique to each individual—also that my faith could restore balance and harmony in my personal relationship with the Divine realm. My inner guidance has always kept me knowing that religion was a great source for worship, and instilling in me strong morals and faith; now it just deepened and connected the dots with what Spirit had shown me.

The valuable lessons that came through from Spirit's guidance to quiet my mind were life shifting, creating openings on many levels. First I came to see how the mini-lifetime movies I was replaying over and over were no longer serving my life.

Then I began the practice of listening while being open-minded. Spending time in silence taught me to hear the tone of Spirit as well as to be comfortable in my own company. I also stopped speaking about the stories that I stayed in so much of the time. When the stories no longer had an energetic life, not only did my inner dialogue change, but my outward conversations did, too. My energy and view began to widen beyond the limitations that Shmego guy had put in place.

I was now able to understand the relationships in my life, which of them could heal by ending them and which ones were awaiting a new beginning. I could also see how inviting new, healthier relationships in could offer new growth. I began to see that I had a pattern of participating in negative relationships that drained my energetic health. I learned and honored the lessons from the relationship before moving out of it, and that offered me healing and growth. Spirit impressed the importance of loving the other person even when his or her actions challenged me, and that taught me to open up to the tone of compassion. A compassionate heart heals the pain. Otherwise, the pain stays on and builds negative energy within the body.

Listening with an open heart to loved ones helped me to see clearly the person I had been while transitioning into the person I was meant to be.

I soon realized through this fantastic first principle of quieting the mind that the gift of a quiet mind invites a whole new view and energetic level to life.

Quieting the Mind

Breath ✿ Awareness of Self ✿ Awareness of Body

When you are learning how to quiet your mind, it is best not to judge your thoughts. Ego will trick you into negative thought patterns. Learning how to keep ego out of your thoughts is a process. It will take some time, but with practice, you will learn when ego is talking and when your Inner Goddess is talking.

There is no right or wrong way to meditate, and there are many different ways to do so, so it may take you awhile to find which form resonates in you.

Sometimes your mind will quiet down without your even realizing it. Other times, it may take a while. Thoughts of the day or a to-do list may pop into your head. If this happens, simply bring your mind back and focus on a breathing technique that I call cycle breathing. Don't panic! A guide for cycle breathing is on the next page. When you feel ego kicking in, don't judge or slip into its ways; just go back to your breath.

Always start in a quiet spot. No phones or TV. Be in the moment. It is easiest to do this as soon as you begin your day or when you end your day. Begin your daily practice of meditation at the same time and in the same place. This will help your body and mind adjust and open with ease. It is best not to hold yourself or the meditation to any standard of expectation. You will be open to receiving the energy the more relaxed you are.

The best cure for the body is a quiet mind.

-Napoleon Bonaparte

Keeping a copy of your journal by your side when you meditate is a good routine to start. You can then write any thoughts that come up. It also gives you a chance to track your progress as you start to turn away from ego thoughts and move toward love thoughts and harmony. You will notice and feel the difference right away.

In both this book and in **The Goddess You Journal**, I ask that you "Nancy Drew it." Dig deep and uncover all the hidden details like any good detective would!

✿ "Nancy Drew it" is a coined phrase by moi. When you "Nancy Drew it," you become a detective by uncovering all the hidden details of the question at hand. Nancy Drew is a fictional teenage girl detective invented by author Carolyn Keene in the 1930s book series by the same name.

Breathing Exercise

Have your journal nearby to record any sensations you notice and any impressions you get.

❀ Begin to cycle breath by inhaling through your nose.

❀ Exhale, with control, through your mouth. When all the air is out, begin again with another inhalation through the nose.

❀ Every time you do this cycle breathing do it with the purpose and intent of filling your lungs and belly with life-force energy on the inhale and releasing all the trapped negative energy on the exhale.

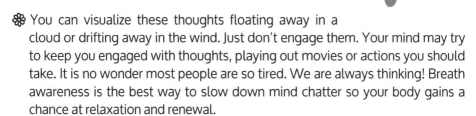

❀ Anytime your mind begins to wander with thoughts or ideas, release any attachment to them and direct your mind back to your breathing and your body.

❀ You can visualize these thoughts floating away in a cloud or drifting away in the wind. Just don't engage them. Your mind may try to keep you engaged with thoughts, playing out movies or actions you should take. It is no wonder most people are so tired. We are always thinking! Breath awareness is the best way to slow down mind chatter so your body gains a chance at relaxation and renewal.

Did you know most people never use their lungs to their full capacity? That is because we tend to breathe shallowly as we attempt to keep up with a face-paced life.

Try the cycle breath when you're stressed or anxious. Do this breath awareness exercise as many times a day as you can.

Ego Shmego

"It is the nature of the ego to take, and the nature of the spirit to share."—Proverb

Remember earlier when I spoke about Ego Shmego? That the Angels had taught me all about fear and ego? Well, let me introduce you to my little "friend" Ego Shmego.

Shmego here is your fear-based thoughts.

Shmego's one and only job in life is to serve you up fear whenever he can.

Shmego is cunning, deceitful and a trickster.

He will and does manipulate your thoughts and make you feel "less than" while hiding the truth from you that you are love.

This is his one and only job so, as you might expect, he is pretty darn good at it.

Shmego is fear, and fear is the opposite of love. Love my friends is the tone of truth: the truth of your soul, the truth of God's unending love for you. The truth is that love can heal your life.

Your Journey Begins with Your First

Action Steps

1. Lay open your journal with two blank pages side-by-side. On one page, (go ahead grab your markers or glitter if you want) label the top "Ego Thoughts"; label the other page "Love Thoughts." For the next week, write down your thoughts on the proper page. By doing this action, we bring awareness to our thought patterns. There is no denying them.

2. Write in your journal how these thought patterns have affected your life. Be sure to "Nancy Drew it."

3. Write yourself a love letter! Include all the juicy details of your self-love!

4. Begin your cycle breathing meditation every day at least twice a day for ten minutes.

5. Follow *The Goddess You Journal* prompts EVERY DAY!

It is important at the start of your Goddess You journey that you learn to recognize Ego Shmego's manipulative patterns. When Shmego rears his ugly head, along with his negative thought patterns, he will try and convince you that you are batshit crazy for thinking you are gifted, intuitive, pretty, deserving, smart, worthy, happy or any other forward-thinking word. Recognizing Shmego's tone will undoubtedly help you know where the love is not present in your life. Love's tone, when ignited, opens your senses to an even deeper connection of love's groovyness and unending energy, while opening the doorway to your Soul Self.

You have to be ready with your brand new arsenal to call Shmego out. So get ready to lock and load, here's your ammo:

When you notice an ego thought, immediately turn it into a love thought—otherwise known as forward-thinking, my friend. Shmego likes you living with a backward view at the past. Forward-thinking and forward-living, on the other hand, are gifts of the present. The present is where God's love resides and fear is not welcome.

Principle Two

Self-Love

Once I began practicing the quiet the mind principle, I noticed that its' energy opened the pathway for a deeper connection to Spirit, thus allowing the spiritual guidance I was receiving to be welcomed and implemented in my life. I was embracing the messages I was receiving, and lovely confirmations came along to reinforce those messages.

During this time, I embraced with a cautious heart the fact that I was indeed more than what my limited thoughts had me believe I was. I say my heart was cautious because with any life change, that Shmego guy will undoubtedly use his negative tone to keep you living with fear. The good news was that I was armed and ready to see Shmego's sneaky little tone behind the thoughts and words that came to mind. I used my tools to shift the low vibrational fear thinking into a higher vibrational love tone. Shmego had nowhere to hide, which made my soul crave more spiritual guidance to keep the awakening coming forth.

Spirit began the next reflection of what I now know as the self-love principle.

Spirit spoke to me through reflections—quite literally. I noticed mirrors everywhere I went. And, by the way, I really fought against the message to see my reflection. I had become so used to seeing myself in a less than loving way that my habit was to look only for what I was lacking—what I was not. I could only see all the imperfections that I was used to complaining about.

Journal Prompt:

What are you seeing in
your reflection?

Spirit's tone speaking of self-love, kept coming to me in mirrors with the clear message that for my life to make any sense, I would have to see myself as God sees me. Spirit's message finally got my attention, and I heard it loud and clear.

Mirrors began to speak tones of Spirit's love reflecting back at me. Spirit's love began filling the void that I had not been aware was there. I saw that I had created a void that existed within me. And that the reflection of self-loathing I was living in had actually been filling the void with low vibrational thoughts, drama relationships, addiction to caffeine, junk foods and wine, to name a few. Yup, I admit it! I was a hot mess. But to some, I appeared to have the perfect life. To myself I thought, "It is true, I do have more than many others, so I should just be happy, Right?" Only I wasn't happy with who I was.

What I did not grasp at the time was that when you are an empath, you can feel these tones from others, and they can become part of who you are if you are not aware of the energy. You become confused about who you are and are not. You can take on personalities and issues that don't belong to you, thinking and feeling that they are your own. This is what Spirit showed me during the self-love lesson. I had become the thoughts and views of others. I took on habits and personality traits of others. I had lost my sense of me.

Similarly, people who are sensitive or empathetic can sometimes become entangled with others' energies as well, leaving them feeling less-than, depleted or even self-loathing.

Journal Prompt:

Are you taking on
others pain, and how?

Spirit's invitation to self-love came in from many directions and in many different forms. Self-love, Spirit taught me, was vital to living in soul alignment. Spirit showed me the reason I was stuck in the swirl of low vibrational living was because I was reflecting out to the world the lower version of myself. This is how Spirit taught me about the mirror effect.

The Mirror Effect

The mirror effect is the reflection of what you put out in energetic tones, meaning your feelings, your thoughts and your views. These reflections then come back to you. This is how we stay in the low vibration of self-sabotaging thinking. These thoughts become an endless circle of energy. To break the cycle of the mirror effect from continuing at a low vibration, Spirit impressed a vision in my mind of my higher self. This view of my higher self was an incredible vision, to say the least. What I had not learned in my life thus far about loving and respecting myself was now coming full force at me. I saw how my lack of love toward myself was like a prison cell that was confining my soul while enabling ego to be in charge.

As I began to change how I saw myself in the mirror, I also began speaking to myself in a loving way. When a problem arose, rather than verbally abusing myself, Spirit guided a new voice of love in.

"See yourself as a reflection of how God sees you." Spirit taught me the mirror lesson, and now I pass it along to you, so you can go right now and look in a mirror and see yourself through God's eyes.

Spirit began to impress the importance of being comfortable in my own presence. I was shown that always being around others left no time for listening to my intuition or to Spirit. This idea was foreign to me as I have always been such a social gal. What I had noticed since practicing the quieting the mind lesson was I felt different, lighter and happier. So I agreed to follow the nudge Spirit led me to spend time alone.

Journal Prompt:

What is your reflection

revealing to you?

I began to take myself to lunch, just me, myself and I, as I would tell my hubby when he would ask with whom I was going out. I started to refer to myself as my own BFF.

Spirit impressed that this was to be time spent alone, and that allowed me to savor the quietness of my being while practicing self-love. On these self-dates, I began to see a new side of myself emerge. I heard my inner tone speak more clearly of things I liked or didn't like. I had been in a routine of not being able to make clear decisions. Spirit impressed that I had lost my connection to knowing my Soul Self. These dates with my Soul Self gave me an opportunity to speak clearly and love my-

self with ease. They also helped me to invite my voice of truth in, to hear the voice of what serves my soul and what does not. Loving myself paved the way for my Soul Self to shine forward. I was taught that our Soul Self can be hidden beneath layers. To live in alignment with our soul, we must honor our self.

You Are Made of Love

Being real is love. Love is the constant. When you give your love to someone, you cannot take it away, for it is already there. You are made of love.

Having self-love is not the same as being conceited or stuck up. Self-love comes from the love of being who you are. Accept that you are worthy of loving yourself. Believe that you are just how God has meant you to be: perfectly you!

Here in your journey, I would like to share the beautiful words of Marianne Williamson:

"Our deepest fear is not that we are inadequate. Our deepest fear is that we are powerful beyond measure. It is our light, not our darkness that most frightens us. We ask ourselves, Who am I to be brilliant, gorgeous, talented, fabulous? Actually, who are you not to be? You are a child of God. Your playing small does not serve the world. There is nothing enlightened about shrinking so that other people won't feel insecure around you. We are all meant to shine, as children do. We were born to make manifest the glory of God that is within us. It's not just in some of us; it's in everyone. And as we let our own light shine, we unconsciously give other people permission to do the same. As we are liberated from our own fear, our presence automatically liberates others. "

Self-love is liberating. When you practice the principle of self-love daily, you become aware of your gifts and learn to accept them. Let go of ego thought patterns that keep you from staying in the light and love. Know that you are exactly how you were meant to be. Without judgment, accept this fact. This is how you will achieve self-love to the fullest.

Cycle Breathing Meditation

Follow the steps for the cycle breathing meditation in chapter one. Your meditation intention is on "love of self." Spend at least ten minutes each day reflecting on this love of you, this pure, unconditional love. Picture the white, loving light of God flowing through your heart, opening it and healing anything that may need healing. Allow your body to release anything that comes up. Do not hold it in or form any judgment. Send only healing, compassionate thoughts as you let go. BE IN THE LIGHT.

"Once you become 'REAL' you can't become unreal again. It lasts for always."

-Margery Williams,
The Velveteen Rabbit

Mirror, Mirror

Leaving yourself love notes on your mirror will help remind you to think and see yourself through

God's loving eyes!

Know that your thoughts about yourself really do matter in how you reflect your light out onto others. You must learn that what you think is mirrored back to you. Your limited love of self and your own greatness hold you back from reaching your true potential, leaving you in a holding pattern.

You know what I am talking about here, don't you?

A change of thought and perception of how you view yourself is in fact, a miracle. This new thought pattern then allows you to see the true beauty of your soul.

In principle one, you learned what Shmego thoughts look like, how they feel and how they affect your life. This shift of thought away from Shmego, which is dark, cold, lonely, fearful, regretful and on and on, is again a miracle! Each and every time you choose love over fear, you become a forward-thinking person.

Forward-thinking is God's light shining through your very being.

God created you with special gifts and talents. Your goal is to embrace that you are unique. Now grab your journal and meet me on the next page.

Self-Love Exercise

Acceptance of Self ❀ *Loving Self* ❀ *Believing in Self*

Your assignment can get a bit emotional, so grab your tissues!

Previously, you were asked to write yourself a love letter. If you did not do this, please take the time to write it before you continue on your Goddess journey. If it's written, awesome! Grab that letter and go to your meditation place.

❀ Do your breathing exercise while holding this letter close to your heart.

❀ Set your intention while you begin to open your heart fully and allow self-love in.

❀ Allow yourself as much time as you need in this exercise to fully absorb love in.

❀ Feel the meaning of this letter soak into your heart.

Intention is your new best friend. Dress her up and take her with you everywhere you go. Set your intentions from moment to moment each day.

Sometimes our thoughts cause roadblocks that prohibit us from receiving love. Whatever the reason for the block, you can work through it with the help and support of self-love.

When you have completed your meditation, grab your Journal and respond to the following prompts:

1. How do you feel at this moment?

2. What sensations (sight, sound, touch, smell, taste) did you notice? You know, "Nancy Drew it."

3. Do you desire more of this love?

4. What is one word you would use to describe your love of self?

5. How do you view yourself?

6. How do you think God sees you?

Soulful Moments

We do not remember days, we remember moments. ~Cesare Pavese

Now that you have the first two tools in the Goddess You principles, you will create soulful moments throughout each day. Your change in thought will shift and so will the people who come into your life. You may also notice people shifting away from you. This is the universe in motion. You are energy based, so as a result, your thoughts emit energy. Without even fully being aware of it, you created the life you are living right now. Amazing, right?

And, are you are ready for more? More joy, more love, more abundance? You are setting the stage, changing the actors, and implementing a brand new script into your life!

You will see more gratitude, and you will feel it, too, with an open loving heart. Journal your gratitude. Be thankful, be grateful, be hopeful, be love!

ACTION STEP TOOL BOX
- FAITH
- PRAYER
- LOVE
- ALLOWING
- JOURNALING
- CONNECTING

Action Steps

Write yourself love notes each day after your meditation. They can be one word or a short sentence. Hold these notes to your heart and allow the vibration of the words to seep in. Hang these notes on your mirror to help you reflect back on this love regularly. Carry the intention of self-love throughout each day.

"My mind, body and soul are connected and aligned with Divine Love."

Journal Prompt:

What shifts have you

noticed in your thoughts?

Principle Three

Changing Your Reactions

The mirror effect of self-love began to shift my life. As I embraced the things I once shunned about myself, a new, lighter energy began to flow. The flow opened new energy pathways within my body. Spirit continued guiding and teaching me how to change my reactions. I was also shown how, by staying in the reactive tone I was living in, I was missing the value of the lesson I could be learning from the present situation.

I am the first to admit that I was living in a feisty, Leo-roaring way. I was hopped up on reacting. Little did I know that those reactions were major, and I mean major, stopping points for living in alignment with the Divine. My Soul Self could not emerge with the fiery reactions going on. I had to tame that lioness and realign her with Divine forces for her own well-being.

Spirit nudged me to change my reactions. Over and over the nudge came. When I would begin to spout out without thinking, the nudge of Spirit's loving tone came in to slow my breath, open my heart and release the thought. Spirit impressed upon me to shift the thought to a tone of compassion, that compassion without compromise was the way to healing the block within my heart. Spirit then showed me the symbol of the heart. It was the heart from a scene of The Wizard of Oz. This heart became the symbol Spirit uses to remind me to open my heart and calm the lioness.

Spirit taught me to listen more and speak less. I spent weeks in silence, only speaking when spoken to. My car rides were meditative and prayer filled. This practice taught me to open to the principle of changing my reactions I practiced compassion without compromise and seeing others with an open heart.

As a result, I stopped reacting in my usual feisty way. Instead, I allowed time to slow down before I spoke. When I did speak, I connected to my heart center, allowing me to really see the other person. This changed my relationships for the better. I learned my reactions were keeping me from seeing other people through God's eyes , and that those reactions I had grown accustom to were what fueled Shmego. The previous principle of self-love taught me to see the God-light within myself, and now I was seeing the very same God-light within others. I began to see their soul energy emerging from behind the barriers they had created to hide from their soul truth. I was now able to recognize how I had always been able to see the light in others and known how to guide them to see their own light.

This was definitely an "aha" moment for me. Knowing that I had been using these gifts that God gave to me all along without realizing it was affirming Spirit's messages. I now know these messages from Spirit are my soul truth.

Spirit also instilled the importance of putting each principle into practice, with the understanding that each principle is equally important on its own. The magic really happens when all the principles are layered with each other, raising the vibrational energy of the soul as they work together to harmonize your life.

Spirit's lesson of changing my reactions led to inviting in others of like mind. I opened up deeper with my fellow Reiki sisters. Each offered her lovely, talented energy to our newfound sisterhood. We began gathering for monthly sharing time, offering each other healing through not only Reiki but also through the many unique gifts we each possess. These sharing times grew our relationships while deepening our faith in the healing work in which we each were venturing. These new relationships led the way for healthier energy and higher vibrational living.

Ellie was one of those new relationships that began during this time. Ellie, with her unwavering faith in God and her Catholic faith, taught Reiki to those who found their way to her. Her faith shines through in the tone in which she teaches. Once you are under her wing of faith, she prepares you for all that God has to offer you. It is not so much the Reiki teachings that stayed with me from that time but the love of God and the Virgin Mother that Ellie so effortlessly brought into each class. The reminder of my own faith was mirrored back to me through this strong and passionate woman. She helped people heal through her connection to the Divine and channeling God's love. Ellie taught me that I, too, was a conduit for love, I just had to choose it, stand in it and believe in it wholeheartedly. It was unwavering faith, pure and simple.

Spirit's lesson: the only thing you have control over is your reaction. That is a big one to swallow for anyone who thinks she can control things. Had I not followed Spirit's guidance to change my reactions, I would never have believed that statement.

During this time, I began to trust in and deliver the messages I was receiving from Spirit in what I call my "blurted readings." I gave one such blurted reading to a woman named Carly, who was about

twenty-three at the time. My tone of delivery, shall we say, was not at its highest vibration yet; however, I did speak directly and honestly about the messages I received .
Because I wasn't fully aligned with Divine Source my delivery lacked the depth of love needed to deliver the message fully, as I guess may be the case for any novice medium. Keep in mind that I have no formal earthly training in mediumship. All my training has come from Spirit's guidance. So Carly's reading started as any conversation naturally does. We were sitting around a table with other fellow Reiki healers in training. Carly, in her sweet voice, asked if any of us could "see" if she and her boyfriend would eventually marry. She was so excited to know if he was "the one," the father of her children, the dream man for whom she had been waiting. The message hit me so fast and hard I nearly burst out of my chair. I repeated what I heard, "No, he is not 'the one.' He is the now, but not the one." She sunk in her chair.

As others consoled her, I questioned the message. Others said, "Yes, he is." I knew in my core that he was not, but how could I relay this to her, now that I'd basically shocked the shit out of her? I learned many valuable lessons from this experience, and the main lesson is that Angels don't lie, and the truth is in the message. Softening my delivery came with practice and compassion. In the end, Carly and her boyfriend parted in the most loving way a relationship could end. They broke up three years after I blurted out that message. I am happy to report that she is in a new relationship with "the one." How do I know? The Angels told me so!

So my friends, I invite you to ask yourself how you could change your everyday, normal response to a different re-action. Can you see your reactions as a vibration instead of an action?

Changing Your Reactions

Lead your day with kind, loving thoughts!

One of the biggest lessons that I have learned over the course of time is that I don't have any control over anyone but myself. Being a stubborn Leo, I love to butt heads with others. It is in my very DNA to roar. I have learned to tame my inner lioness, to get along better with others, to not bite their heads off with my words or tone of voice. This was not an easy feat!

How did I tame her? The most important question is: Why did my lioness need to be tamed? As I began my spiritual awakening, unveiling my Inner Goddess, Spirit led me to see that I was causing the drama in my life. Drama is Shmego's way of manipulating our thoughts into believing, "I am right. I need to be heard. The other people are crazy. It is all about me!"

When we shift our view off of "me" and focus on love, it is a miracle moment. Our thoughts of self turn to compassion for others. We can lead our day with kind, loving thoughts. When confronted with an argument, we choose not to react to the actions or words of the other person. We slow down, hear what the other person is saying (while not taking their words or negativity to heart) and release any attachment to their statement from our being. We start to see a pattern playing out. That person needs to be heard.

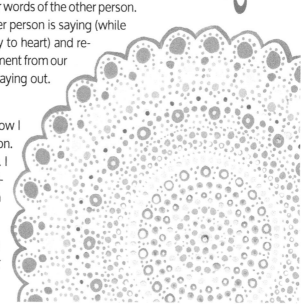

I used to react impulsively, but now I change my reaction to a love action. I do not play into Shmego's game. I rise above and stand in my true Goddess Self. I see that person through the eyes of compassion and love.

The "how" is now part of the "why," you see? It all fits together like a nice little puzzle.

Shut Your Lips

Silence is golden!

It's a cliché, but I must tell you that when I first started to put into practice the idea of "silence is golden," I immediately found amazing results when I shut my lips. When I stopped my reacting to the average, everyday spat with my hubby and started to pray for him and for the situation at the time, I found that putting it in God's precious hands always worked. I did not have to blow my top, roar my roar or defend my mark. It seemingly just got better. It's as simple as a prayer and a release.

Now of course this was not easily understood by my main squeeze because, honestly, he was feeding off my crazy lioness ways, and I was feeding off of his ways. When I made the intention (there it is again, intent!) to change the craziness and drama, it was like the Fairy Godmother Goddess within me came to life. Just like that, I waved my magic wand, set my intent, and things were magically transformed.

So dig out your wand, dust it off and get to work!

Keep Your Chatter to a Minimum

Silence is the sleep that nourishes wisdom. ~Francis Bacon

This assignment will be challenging but very rewarding. It is time to sit in silence for a week.

What do I mean exactly?

No radio, no TV, no long phone chats, no texting conversations and no social media. This should be a week dedicated to embracing the sounds around you, to hearing what others are saying and to really listening to your soul.

If you are like me, then you tend to move so quickly throughout your day that you really end up missing a lot. By allowing the mind to have a break from the nonstop action that you force-feed it daily, your mind gets to rest. Your mind can then open pathways that promote new growth, new thought patterns and new insights. Now, of course, you will have to speak to answer questions and whatnot. Just keep your chatter to a minimum. Having no radio or TV will also lead the way to connecting with your Inner Goddess and heighten your intuition. Trust me on this!

As hard as it may seem to stop your chatter, to not jam out to your favorite tunes while you drive, text your BFF or watch your favorite show, you will soon see a new sense of peace and calm that you have not noticed in a long time!

Your Mission

Awareness Challenge

Your Challenge:

❀ Think before you speak.

❀ Stop the chatter and outside noise.

❀ Use your magic to change your normal reaction.

❀ No text, phone, TV or social media.

Journal each day about the following:

❀ What does it feel like today to be quiet?

❀ What you are hearing?

❀ How have you changed your reaction(s) to certain people or situations?

❀ How is your intuition opening?

Journal Prompt:

How are you feeling?

What are the biggest

changes you

have noticed?

Take time now to reflect on these questions. Go ahead, journal them!

Now it's time to put the lessons together:

Principle One: *Quieting your mind*

Principle Two: *Self-love*
(opening your heart to love yourself)

Principle Three: *Change your reactions*
(putting an end to your reactions to others)

Each of these principles open your heart to be more compassionate. Your thoughts will grow, and as that inner chatter slows down, you open your whole being. You will allow that beautiful voice of your Inner Goddess Soul Self to sing her song!

Keep the calm and carry on.

Action Steps

Goddess Mission Challenge

1. Follow the challenge list for at least one week.

2. Record your findings in your journal.

Principle Four

Energy Basics

As I began to change my reactions, I noticed shifts in my body. The shifts were in a certain, noticeable energetic tone. My body was releasing old blocks I had created with low vibrational living and thinking. This is when Spirit began to guide me in understanding the importance of energy and how it works.

I had previously learned about energy centers within the body and around the body—chakra centers, as they are commonly known, and the aura, the energy that surrounds your being. Spirit took this basic knowledge to a new level of understanding while teaching me the importance of energy basics.

Spirit taught that we are all made up of energy. Our energy flow reflects the health of our mind, body and soul. The soul is perfect energy with a connection to the Divine as the spiritual lifeline. The seat of the soul, which Spirit impressed upon me, is in the heart center, known as the heart chakra. The top of the head, or crown chakra, is where the Divine meets our being.

Spirit taught me during this time how each energy center must be cleaned of blocks and debris caused by life events, pains and sufferings that occur to teach us valuable lessons. When we are unable to see the lesson in the life event or when we hold on to pain or suffering, our energy can become blocked.

Once blocked, that energy vibrates at a lower rate. Over time the lower the vibrational rate, the more debris that builds up, the more our well-being is affected.

Icky Cobwebs

Spirit showed me how I had been picking up others' icky cobwebs of energy. These cobwebs are low vibrational energy. Spirit taught me the importance of clearing this energy while inviting in angelic help. Angels, when called upon, will assist in restoring balance. This angelic help will transform low vibrational energy into loving high vibrational energy.

This was not the first time I had been shown angelic energy. As a matter of fact, years earlier I avoided this information. I read books on connecting to the Angels in the early 1990s, but I shrugged them off. My fearful thinking kept me from embracing the angelic realm. Thankfully, here was the tone again. This time I listened with an open mind and heart.

Spirit guided me to the Archangels. I spent meditative time in communion with the Divine realm. As I began to clear the energy around me and within my being, I noticed a huge shift in my well-being. The pathways to the chakras began to release, restoring balance in my energetic body. Not only did I notice a big difference in energy and focus, but others began to take notice as well. My home and family were now also benefiting from the energy shift.

Spirit led me into a meditation where I was taught to open each chakra energy center, invite the Angels and Archangels to come clear and balance each chakra while reconnecting each center to the Divine.

This practice of energy balancing is something I now use each and every day.

The Energy of Food

Spirit's teachings on energy also led me to understand how the vibration of food affects our energy systems. Maintaining a high vibrational body requires equally high vibrational food. The lesson of holding energy came forward.

Spirit taught me how to hold energy within the palms of my hands. To start, I was guided to hold my hands together in prayer pose while connecting to the energy of my being. Slowly moving the hands further apart, I still felt the energy. Go ahead and try this!

Once the connection to the energy of my being was established, Spirit guided me in moving my hands around my body to feel the energy at different points. I used my journal to jot down the feeling along with the tones I felt. Next, I moved to feeling the energy of objects and food.

Because everything is made up of energy, you can tune in to that energy for insight. For instance if I was working on my diet, I would hold the item of food in my hand to get a sense of its energetic tone. I could then understand if that food would serve my energetic body and how.

This opened me to a whole new level of energy practice. Not only could I personally benefit from this energy technique, but I could also now help "know" what energies would best serve my clients' well-being. Not only in food, but also in many other areas of life such as relationships, house clearings, jobs, money and so on.

My Molly

It was around this same time as well that my youngest daughter, Molly, was struggling in school with class work and relationships. It really started back in the seventh grade with some kids bullying Molly. At the time, I was really being drawn to move her out of the public school she was in, and I had even set up some private school tours. I was not fully feeling the change of school yet, so we ended up letting go of the idea of a move.

In the meantime, we worked on Molly's strengths—acting, singing and dancing. I also worked with her on guiding her to be strong in her tone. The problem was that she was absorbing others' behaviors and did not understand what was going on. By the time she was in high school, Molly continued to struggle with her identity and experienced more bullying. We tried to help her to not blame others and stand strong in herself, while also not dismissing the bullying. That's hard to do without blaming and causing more stress.

During Molly's sophomore year, the bullying became worse. What seemed like normal girl stuff was turning into a dangerous time. Molly began picking up the darker traits of her peers, and being an empath, she had not yet learned how to protect herself from others' energy. She did not yet understand what was hers and what was another person's.

Around this time, Molly started having dreams of a woman we had known who had taken her own life in her thirties. Her name was Margo, and when she was alive, she had been fond of visiting me at my shoe store. She would stay and talk with Molly and me for the longest time. We also knew Margo from our family's favorite restaurant, where Margo worked. Molly was unsettled about her dreams, and then the experience moved into clairvoyance, where Molly was seeing Margo during the day. Molly would say, "I just saw Margo in a cab." That may seem eerie, but I knew that Margo was trying to help Molly understand when she was taking on other people's energy as an empath. Margo was a beautiful woman whose smile and light I can still feel.

Spirit was speaking to me in new ways at this time, and I started to receive stronger signals. The signs they sent were amazing and accurate. Margo came to me as well; I knew there was a connection now. Being an empath, I had sensations of pain and depression. I knew this to be Molly. Spirit was guiding both of us at the same time. The day the truth came to me was in a sign from Spirit and a message.

The signs had been all around. The number 26 was the strongest and seemed to appear anywhere a number was displayed. That number is what I see when my husband's Gammy comes through. I also see a multitude of ladybugs as another confirmation that Gammy is present and guiding in spirit. She was strong and loud in her tone when I finally listened! She sent another of my friends to pass a verbal message to me: "Spirit will really work hard at aiding us. We just need to be open." I had been trying so hard to figure out what was going on that I needed a "voice" to guide me! This friend looked upset and asked if she could speak to me about something important so she and I sat inside my car. When my friend spoke, the knowing came through loud and clear! I knew what must be done. I had a mission, so I asked my friend to get out of the car, knowing that more talking would only keep the energy perpetuating. I knew that I had to move quickly.

Immediately, I called our doctor's office, then the school, then my husband. I explained to them what my friend had just confirmed for me that Molly had been cutting herself and needed help. When I picked Molly up, we talked for a few minutes. She confirmed that she had been cutting and showed me her arm and upper leg. We drove off while I held in my tears. I prayed and asked the Angels to stay by our sides and to guide me in knowing what to do.

As soon as we got to the doctor's office, the Angels came through. They told me to get her B-12 level checked. When I asked for blood work, and specifically vitamin B-12, the doctor said that it would not be necessary because typically only the elderly have low B-12. The Angels pushed me, so I asked again. After a few more debates, the doctor agreed, and ordered the necessary blood work.

We also talked about antidepressants because Molly wanted to go on them. I knew this was another empath pickup she had. One of her friends was cutting, and another friend was on antidepressants. I was able to talk her out of the idea of medication just yet. We agreed to go and see a therapist so Molly could work through this major life event with a trained professional.

The call from the doctor came twenty-four hours later. She said Molly's B-12 number was so low that she was shocked. She had never seen a teenager's levels that low. Spirit came through again with the message to bring her to another doctor who practiced functional medicine so we could have more tests done. I made an appointment with that doctor right away.

The new doctor ran several other tests, one of which told us that Molly would never absorb B-12; she would have to have B-12 injections for the rest of her life.

Thank you, Angels, for that guidance!

The following October during her junior year, after several more bullying incidents and disruptive events, I met with the school to talk about how to best deal with these personal attacks. We talked about social media and how the kids use it to live a life of false or grandiose views. We discussed the issues about texting and the fact that it is easy to type words to someone and not have the person right in front of you for a response. Tone, feeling and personalities are lost with texting. I then told the school about that fact that I had encouraged Molly to delete those "friends" who were doing the bullying from her phone.

The school agreed with the steps we had taken and offered a few options to help the situation. I knew their suggestions would only make the situation grow worse so I continued to follow Spirits guidance.

Making Molly delete these friends from her phone was like pulling teeth. She was fighting having to face the fact that these so-called friends were hurting her and causing her pain and suffering. The final push was a text she received from a few so-called pals: A list in which they included the top things they hated about Molly. She was devastated. After I calmed her down and assured her that those words were not who she was, she agreed and finally deleted them from her phone and social media accounts.

By November, the Angels were at it again, showing me signs of Molly in a new school. My husband and I attended my nephew's play at his private high school around this time. As soon as we took our seats, my husband and I exchanged glances. "This is where Molly needs to be," my husband said. That night, we asked Molly if she would like to go to this new school. Without any hesitation, she said yes!

Molly started in January of her junior year. The transition was smooth, and her academics improved, far beyond her, or our, expectations. We saw this as another confirmation of how painful life had become for her in the old school. Molly had learned how her gift of being an empath can be burdensome but also valuable. She learned that clearing and protecting herself are as important as her B-12 shots.

My girl is now an amazing young college woman, ready to take on the world with her talents and gifts. She has healthier friendships while staying true to herself. Margo still "visits" Molly every now and then, reminding Molly to stand in her light and to take her B-12 shot.

Thanks, Margo!

Energy Basics

God is life-force energy. Energy is constant.

I repeat. God is life-force energy. Energy is constant.

It is always in motion and ever changing. We are all energy beings. We emit energy from our chakra centers.

Have you ever had a flashback to a moment in time? Did you have a strong feeling in your body that reminded you of that moment? Your body holds energy from past events, illnesses, emotional wounds and much more. Earth is energy. Even material things are made up of energy.

Understanding the basics of your energy being is a crucial step on your spiritual journey as you connect to your Inner Goddess.

Energy and its effect on you can be explained as simply as this:

❀ Food and water are energy for your body, mind and soul. Fill your body with good nutrition, and you experience good results; put lower energy or low vibrational food in, get lower body energy, sluggishness, moodiness, poor digestion and more.

❀ How you react creates energy. Calm reactions keep your body on an even keel. But a crazy reaction raises your blood pressure, pushing your fight-or-flight response to an extremely high level. This causes tension, stress or even bitterness to be born as a result of these negative reactions.

❀ Your thoughts create some of the strongest forms of energy. Karma is an outcome of your thinking and actions. What you think comes back to you. Simply stated, what goes around comes around.

✿ The people with whom you spend your time impact your energy. Surround yourself with positive, happy and upbeat individuals who want to see you succeed, and you'll feel the beauty in the energy that will follow that choice. Spending time with someone who is moody, gossipy or always complaining will leave you always feeling depleted rather than lifted.

✿ How you spend your time creates certain energies. Serving others with your talents, walking your spiritual path, giving and loving—will prove to be uplifting. But getting caught up in keeping up with the Joneses or getting addicted to computers, drugs, alcohol, sex or even your cellphone can leave you depleted, tired, moody and low, low, low!

Icky, Sticky Cobwebs

Wherever you go, no matter what the weather, always bring your own sunshine.

~Anthony J. D'Angelo

Another key aspect regarding energy is knowing that you are energy. Understand that people carry their energy wherever they go. They can, in fact, leave some behind for you. Have you ever just randomly noticed someone and sensed something was up with that person? Good or bad? You, without even realizing it, take it home and share that mess with your loved ones.

Yikes, what a load of crappy energy to dump on others!

There are several ways to help raise your energy and vibration and clear away lower energy from your home, space or belongings. No matter the method you use for the clearing, it must always start with intent. Intent and prayer open your energy centers to receiving new, positive energy flow.

Intent and prayer open your connection to higher power and allow you to hear, know, sense, feel and see what needs clearing.

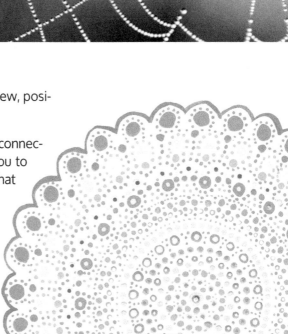

Space Clearing 101

Your sacred space is where you can find yourself again and again. ~Joseph Campbell

To do a basic clearing, start with a sage smudge stick. Sage is known for being a sacred smoke that has been used for thousands of years to help smudge, or move, the lower energy out of the intended area. You can also use Sage-Off, a smokeless smudge spray that I make with pure theraputic grade essential oils and infused with Spirits loving energy through prayer and intent. You can find these high vibrational sprays on my website at - www.jeannestreet.com.

The best place to start clearing space is in your home or the space in which you work. You won't believe the difference when you start with a clean home, free of extra things lying around. For me personally, I like to do a spring-like cleaning the day before. I straighten closets and drawers, and I donate old belongings to charity or to someone I know who could use the items. You can even sell the items to create space for money to flow into your life. Always ask that the energy be recycled and renewed into new higher energy.

Shopping List

- Bags or boxes to pack up old belongings

- Cleaning supplies

- Sage smudge stick

- Smokeless smudge spray

- Lighter

- Abalone shell, clay pot or ashtray (for smudge stick)

- Lavender spray

- Feather (optional)

- Kosher salt

Your Mission: "Clear your Space"

Set your intention and sight ahead on a date to complete your mission!

1. Meditate.

2. Gather your sage and other items needed from the "shopping list."

3. Clean out those closets and drawers—you know it feels good! Have fun with this!

4. Lighten your load by donating, selling or giving away items you no longer need or use.

5. Set your intention for your clearing.

6. Write your prayer to God and the Angels.

Ready. Set. Clear away!

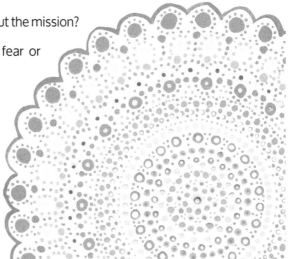

Journal! Take some time to write in your journal before you clean your closets and home.

1. How are you feeling about the mission?

2. Are your feelings from fear or from love?

3. What are your main concerns about the mission?

4. How can you turn your fears or concerns into a new thought pattern?

How to Clear Space

Energy flows where intention goes. ~Unknown

Start by opening a few windows and doors. It's very important that you allow fresh air in, for this will help the smudge smoke flow out. Warning: be careful not to set off your smoke alarms!

❀ Begin at your front or main doorway. Light the smudge stick and gently blow the flame out, or begin spraying your smokeless smudge spray.

❀ Using your hand or a feather, waft the smoke all around the doorway. Always sweep down and away.

❀ Work your way through your home. Open any cabinets, drawers and closets. Leave no corner left un-smudged!

❀ Waft the smoke or spray in every space you can. Move quickly, but with purpose!

❀ Notice any items that seem to be calling to you to clear them.

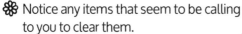

❀ You may need to relight your smudge stick along the way, so keep that lighter handy.

❀ End back at your front door where you began. When I am done smudging my space, I walk back through with lavender spray. I do this to invite new, positive growth into the space I just cleared. Fresh On Lavender Spray is a high-vibration energy source. I keep a bottle in almost every room of my home.

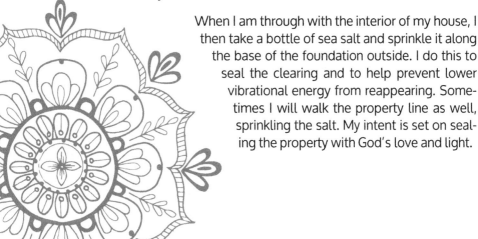

When I am through with the interior of my house, I then take a bottle of sea salt and sprinkle it along the base of the foundation outside. I do this to seal the clearing and to help prevent lower vibrational energy from reappearing. Sometimes I will walk the property line as well, sprinkling the salt. My intent is set on sealing the property with God's love and light.

Mission Accomplished

Nothing builds self-esteem and self-confidence like accomplishment. ~Thomas Carlyle

After your clearing, get back to your journal and respond to the following prompts.

(Be sure to "Nancy Drew it" all the juicy details!)

- ❀ How did you feel during the clearing?
- ❀ How did you start? How did you end?
- ❀ What happened during the clearing?
- ❀ How does your space feel?
- ❀ How are others reacting to your space after the clearing?

Principle Five

Healing the Block

The messages deepened now with the connection to the Angels. Not only was I receiving Spirit's impressions and tone, but the Angels also took the messages to a deeper soul connection. As I began to release my blocks, the Angels taught me that to every healing, there are even more layers within that one healing. Like an onion, some layers are sweet; some make you cry, while other layers take your breath away. The lesson Spirit taught is that healing the block is key in moving forward and living in Divine alignment.

Spirit showed me that within my energy centers, even though I thought I had put something behind me, energy remained that required healing. This meant I still had my work cut out for me.

Healing the block, Spirit impressed over and over, is the only way to free the energy. Without freeing the energy, I would stay perpetually the same. Growth can only come when there is a clear pathway in your energy system. Growth is also a must so you can achieve your soul's work.

Spirit was loud and clear on how to clear the blocks. Again I had this message come to me years before. The difference was that now I understood the depth of the message.

Forgiveness, as you have no doubt learned at some point in your life, is what sets you free. Of course that statement seems so cliché, and its energy then becomes low vibrational. I noticed how most people tend to stay away from clichés and low vibrational tones. So, it's no wonder that the practice of forgiveness is not seen as a valuable tool. Spirit has shown me in numerous ways that the very act of forgiveness actually brings forth your Soul Self. Spirit shines a light that illuminates all the layers of the unforgiving and the resisting— all your responses to events that have festered within you. Beneath that lies the miracle of forgiveness.

Journal Prompt:

Are you a hoarder of

resentments, blame or other

events that keep stuck energy

dwelling in your being?

I found that I was a hoarder in a sense, keeping the blocks of these forgotten energetic tones within my energy system.

Spirit's lesson of healing the block hit me like a ton of bricks. I was under the impression that I had already let go of the past mumbo jumbo, that I moved out of yucky relationships with kindness. But what I learned is that I had not taken the time to open the compassion without compromise and forgive myself as well as others. Now the previous lessons really took on a deeper meaning. I could see the anger and resentment I held onto deep within my energy centers. I noticed that the forgiveness did not always have to make sense to me; sometimes it was the act of prayer that shifted the energy. Having the Angels by my side made these painful and sometimes sorrowful times shift quickly to high vibrational healing.

Spirit taught me that whenever I struggled with an issue I could call for assistance through angelic connection. Spirit now guides me to helping others see that the messages that lead to healing connection are available for everyone. Forgiveness and compassion without compromise are gifts that heal the soul.

The Moral Compass

The value of this important principle came into action during a reading for a dear friend who was struggling from a deception from her then-husband. Stacy and I met a couple of years earlier while she was on her honeymoon, and I was on a winter getaway. We became immediate friends. Well, not exactly immediate. It did take her throwing, I mean spilling, a glass of champagne on me. But that is a whole other story.

It all started with a text. I received a message from Spirit about a man who I knew that was connected to Stacy, but I was unsure how. So I sent her a text saying, "Can we talk?" When we got on the phone, I was able to deliver this message that had come randomly to me. It was a male who was coming through, showing me a compass. He was showing me a sign of a compass then saying it was a moral compass and that it was pointing in the wrong direction. As Stacy and I spoke, the man coming through revealed that he was her husband's brother. She did not fully understand the message but thought it might have something to do with her husband's son.

A few months later, I got a call from Stacy telling me of her marriage breakup. I reminded her as she was crying to me about her husbands betrayal and failing marriage that we had received a message from Spirit just months earlier about a moral compass being off, we were both taken back for a moment. What she thought had been a message about her husband's son was actually about her husbands moral compass being off, she just hadn't made the connection yet. I worked with Stacy over the course of her divorce with Spirit's loving guidance and gentleness. She was able to navigate through some very difficult issues. Stacy learned the importance of clearing her space. It was a powerful lesson about the nature of her inner strength and the insight that our loved ones can guide us through the darkest moments, even from heaven, if we are open to receiving. We worked on how her forgiveness and letting go would lead to her healing. In our readings, Spirit reminded Stacy of her faith and God's undying love for her. Stacy was able to exit the marriage in a dignified, loving manner—another testament that God's love prevails through difficult times.

Healing the Block

Do not judge, and you will not be judged. Do not condemn, and you will not be condemned. Forgive, and you will be forgiven. ~Luke 6:37

The act of forgiveness changes the energy and its flow in your body. This increases the vibration of the area in which a block had been formed from what or who you needed to forgive. Understanding how the body is affected by the choices you have made can be an awakening within itself. Through my experience as a medium and a spiritual healer, I have witnessed many clients suffer from disease, low energy levels, constant illnesses, depression and many other life problems that can all be slowly lifted and eventually healed.

All healing stems from the main act of forgiveness. For most people, having a healer work with them to aid in their healing of those areas is very helpful. I have found a few people can do the healings for themselves with constant, dedicated meditation, energy work and a proper diet. Knowing how and when to get help is an important step in learning to connect and listening to your Inner Goddess.

I think that if God forgives us, we must forgive ourselves. Otherwise, it is almost like setting up ourselves as a higher tribunal than Him.

-C. S. Lewis

Forgiveness Is the Healing for Your Soul

Let go of all your pain. May your heart be open to healing. ~Lailah Gifty Akita

Holding on to the past will never let you truly live in the present. Past resentments, judgments and anger will keep you in a stagnant state of being. Not forgiving can lead you down a lonely path to places you really do not want to go. Slowly, you become a person you thought you would never be.

No matter who or what the forgiveness is for, whether it be a life event, past trauma, another person or yourself (let's just call the event a block for simplicity reasons), forgiveness will "heal" the block, the wound and even the pain that you carry from that moment. It is important to understand that forgiveness does not undo the wrongdoing, but it does set you free from the block. Judgments of others will keep you from moving forward.

Intuitive journaling is done when you allow all your senses to flow.

Dance as though no one is watching
Love as though you've never been hurt
Sing as though no one can hear you
Live as though heaven is on earth

True forgiveness only comes when your intent is set on releasing all the ties you have to that block. Release the block to God, the Angels or your higher power. It's simple. Every time you offer forgiveness, you are allowing God to heal your soul. It allows your life to become filled with more love, joy and abundance. Your Inner Goddess will shine like the brightest star. You will feel different—lighter than you have felt in a long time. People will start to notice that you look and seem different. New pathways will begin to open; and healing relationships begin to develop. Your whole energy morphs into a higher vibration.

Shmego can sneak in and have you think you are weak if you forgive.

Shmego, remember, likes you to live in fear. When you choose love over fear, Shmego slips out the back door. Love is the one constant in all things. Love is never ending. The moment in which you doubt love is when Shmego sneaks right back in. You must be mindful of your thoughts and actions and be sure that they are coming from love.

A Clearing

Now that you have done some great energy work and lifted a heavy block, it is time to move the energy. We do this for a couple of reasons. One reason is to clear away the old energy. The second is to raise our own energy levels. We can accomplish this by doing a clearing of the area where we meditate. I love my Sage-Off spray for these times. It is quick and easy. Now the next thing to do is turn on some great music and get your karaoke on! Grab your mic, crank your tunes and dance, dance, dance. Feel your Inner Goddess rock out. Singing, dancing and listening to music helps move energy and raise our vibrations. So get your dance party on!

From my angelic guidance, I have learned that in most cases, we have ignored that the block actually exists, or we believe that we have already worked through that block and have moved on. The truth is that the block is the "onion"; it has many layers. Each time you heal a layer through forgiveness, you are set free from that one layer.

It is a very big concept to grasp. Why would you need to continue to heal the same block in different layers? It is because each time you are brought back to that block, you look at it from a new perspective. Each and every time, you are shown a new view of what healing still needs to take place.

Action Steps

Practicing the act of forgiveness:

❀ Do a space clearing.

❀ Continue to meditate and journal each day.

Journal prompts (be sure to answer with your "Nancy Drew it" hat on):

❀ Write about your current practice of forgiveness.

❀ Who needs your forgiveness?

❀ What needs your forgiveness?

❀ Why do you need to forgive?

❀ What "where's" and "when's" in your life need your forgiveness?

❀ Write about any struggles you may have with a particular forgiveness?

❀ What changes have you noticed about your practice of forgiveness?

❀ How do you feel when you forgive?

Principle Six

Let It Go

A major shift came when Spirit guided me to let it go. This seemed so simple, yet I noticed how Shmego sneaked back in to trick me into holding on to these stories. With every release of memory or block it was time for me to let go of the energy embedded in my body. Shmego, of course, wanted me to hold these stories and pains and keep them close by, just in case.

Thankfully, the previous lesson kicked in as I began to recognize the tone of Shmego while Spirit guided me to see the freedom that would come from just letting go.

I had the false sense that I was those stories. I had relived them, spoke them, dreamed about them for many years. Spirit showed me that these stories not only held me back but also held a connection to others involved in the stories.

This information was really hard to grasp at first. I mean, if I had physically moved on from a yucky relationship, how did the story or truth of it still keep us connected? Spirit answered this with the tone of "karma." Karma is the energy of what you put forth, you get back. The mirror effect again! So this karmic mirror effect, Spirit impressed upon me, was why I was unable to move forward from these stories and people. The constant energy I reflected outward was returning back to me. Yikes! I really had to stop replaying these stories and let them go! Spirit had impressed the importance of intention. Intention, as it was shown to me, is the gas that makes the engine go. Intention is how to get the goal accomplished. Spirit also impressed the importance of having a high vibrational intention.

"How do I make my intention high vibrational?" I asked Spirit in meditation. By inviting the Angels in with your intent, this is God's will: that you have help when you need it. That was the answer I received in meditation. Angels are God's worker bees. You need to just ask for help, and they are there.

Letting go of the stories that I held onto opened a deeper faith and connection to Spirit. Those stories that I thought I owned and had to keep were actually blocking the channels in which I could communicate with Spirit. This was the first time I could ask a question and receive the answer! Although I had previously been under the impression that messages from Spirit were only to be received. I was now able to communicate back and forth with the Divine realm by asking direct questions and receiving specific answers. This was exciting, yet emotional as well. I realized I had been harboring these stories that I thought made me who I was, only to find out those stories actually kept me from being one with my higher self or Soul Self. This is when Spirit guided me to another layer of letting go. I learned that release is symbolic, and when we allow ourselves to flow with the feelings of the release, we can then see the symbolic meaning behind that which we are letting go. For instance, when I let go of the story of me when I was a young girl and I saw people in my room at night, I learned that although these visits turned into a fear for me, it also taught me a valuable tool. It taught me how to go within like the revolving door to shut off the connection to Spirit. My revolving door technique is how I disconnect now from this spiritual work. Without this system of disconnecting I set up as a child, I would be bombarded by Spirit's nonstop messages, just like when I was young. So you can see that this really did turn out to be a miracle for my well-being.

The let it go principle allowed me to then go even deeper to understand that it is part of my journey to remember my gift and find my way back to it. All the life that was built on top of the story had to slowly and carefully be healed, so this new way of living could be revealed. Only then could it be understood on a soul level.

Letting it go gave way for my soul to then come forward in my being. Life began to make sense on a whole new level that I instinctively knew was my soul path.

Signs that your soul is not forward in your being: a.k.a., you're wearing an "Edgar suit." Grab your journal and record any of the following that resonate with you.

Journal Prompt:

Write about something you
have let go of and how the
release brought your
life a miracle.

- Life goes from event to event without the feeling of joy.
- You feel lost, worried, shameful, even lonely around others.
- You don't have a strong sense of your talents.
- You experience self-loathing.
- You feel weak.
- Your mind is scattered.

Keep in mind - These are just some of the traits of a person not living fully in soul alignment.

Holding onto anger is
like grasping a hot coal
with the intent of throwing it at
someone else: you are the one
who gets burned.
~Buddha

How to Let It Go

Life is a succession of lessons which must be lived to be understood. ~Ralph Waldo Emerson

One of the hardest things to do on your spiritual journey is learning how to let go. You hold your "stories" of the past very close and very secure. These stories can be replayed in your mind like a Lifetime miniseries, and you are the lead actress.

Those stories are hard to let go for most of us. On some level in your mind, you believe that the stories make you who you are. When in reality, the stories are just passages to where you are, not who you are. The stories can be ties to the past. In the healing world, these ties can be seen as chains that hold us in a perpetually negative state of being, never really moving forward. These chains can be heavy and cumbersome loads that can prove to be exhausting. You cling to frustration and worry about the past and the future, while not living in the present. These stories can create stress in your body, which in turn can lead to health issues, complicated relationships and other life challenges. You somehow start to surrender to this lifestyle. When doing so, without even being conscious of it, you lose sight of the dreams you once held so dear.

Eckhart Tolle, spiritual teacher and author of The Power of Now and other books, believes that, "we create and maintain problems because they give us a sense of identity. Perhaps this explains why we often hold onto our pain far beyond its ability to serve us."

Letting go can really free you from the past while allowing your Inner Goddess to shine through. Letting go of the control you think you have over these events is so freeing it will make you want to sing out loud with love and compassion. See others through God's eyes and your life will unfold before you as you always dreamed it would.

Get Your Queen Goddess On

Love yourself first and everything else falls into line. You really have to love yourself to get anything done in this world. ~Lucille Ball

Grab your Journal and be the queen of your life.

Write down those stories that you have held onto so tightly. Don't judge them; don't judge any of the characters in them, simply write your truth. Keep the flow of this journal going all week. It does not matter if these entries reflect long, short, big or small moments—just release them.

At the end of the week, take a look over the stories you wrote down. Tear out the pages on which the stories have been written.

Set up a time for a ceremonial fire circle. Go ahead, grab your crown and dress up like a queen as you honor your Inner Goddess.

For your ceremony, have your torn out pages from your Journal, some sage (to burn in the flames), and any other items you feel would be helpful. I like to bring my religious medals and some crystals for spiritual support.

Call in your angels to support your ceremony, add music to set the perfect mood. Build a small fire outside your house. For safety reasons, have some water close by.

Say a prayer before you burn those stories. Let them all go! Witness the flames dancing, sending your stories up to the heavens.

Celebrate like the royal Queen you are!

Action Steps

Release with intention whenever you can.

❀ Any physical action you do can be a release if you set the intention.

❀ Other forms of releasing include: crying, hugging, laughing, singing, writing, drawing, painting, cooking, gardening.

Journal about your ceremony.

❀ What did you notice?

❀ How did it feel to watch the stories turn into flames?

Principle Seven

Chakra Basics

Once I began the practice of letting it go, I noticed my energetic body needed some tending to. All this free space was now in motion, yet not exactly flowing in the right direction. This is when Spirit took the energy lesson a bit further to explain the principle of chakra basics.

Spirit guided me to a meditation in which my energy was purified. During my meditation, I was led to a Divine healing room where I was taught how to open each main chakra and align that chakra to God's Divine energetic flow.

Then I was shown by Spirit that the order in which I cleared and opened the chakras was not as important as making sure each chakra was then connected to the Divine.

Chakra Basics

The body never lies. ~Martha Graham

What is a chakra?

Chakras are energy centers within your body. Chakras are channels where life-force energy flows. Chakras are taught in many religions and cultural backgrounds, so each teacher has his or her own way of teaching about the chakra energy system. I will discuss the seven major chakra centers.

I have studied many different teachings on chakras, and I am constantly learning through my connection to Spirit. When guiding you, my teaching of the chakras will be combined with information from what I have read, what I know intuitively and what the Angels have taught me. There are many layers to these teachings, just as there are many layers to healing.

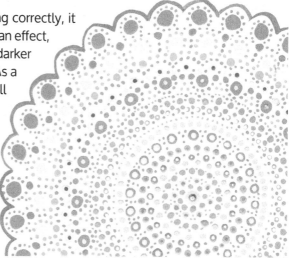

Healthy chakras spin clockwise, quickly without interruption. Each chakra center is associated with the region of the body where it is located. Each chakra within the human body also develops fully at certain ages.

When a chakra is not functioning correctly, it will emit a lower vibration, and as an effect, the color will change to a dull or darker version of the main chakra color. As a result of a blocked chakra, we will see lower energy flow in the area. After extended periods of time, this block may then lead to pain and disease.

The Seven Main Chakras

First Chakra: Root or Base Chakra

Located at the base of your spine, this chakra vibrates to the note of C and emits the color red. This is the first chakra to develop. It is associated with the lower spine, lower female/male organs, hips, legs, feet and adrenals. The root's prime functions are grounding and security. Survival and primal energy are its main issues. Anxiety is a common result of a blocked root chakra. Hip, knee and leg issues can also develop from a blocked root chakra. Additionally, fear is also associated with this chakra.

Second Chakra: Sacral Chakra

This chakra is located just below your naval. It vibrates to the note of D and emits the color orange. The sacral chakra is associated with the lower organs, your sexuality and creativity. Your lower abdomen, urinary track, lower intestines and female/male organs are all associated with the sacral chakra. Intimacy, letting go and emotional needs are a few of the main issues of the sacral chakra.

Third Chakra: Solar Plexus Chakra

The solar plexus is located above your navel, just below the rib cage. It vibrates to the note of E and emits the color yellow. The solar plexus is associated with the digestive system, stomach, liver, small intestines and pancreas. The main issues of the solar plexus are our willpower, self-control and desire. Physical aspects of this chakra are your gut instinct, intuition and the vital energy of your body.

Fourth Chakra: Heart Chakra

Located in the center of your chest, the heart chakra vibrates to the note of F and emits the color green. The heart is your center of giving and receiving love. Emotional balance, heart, lungs, blood pressure, circulation, thymus gland and lymph are its physical properties. The main issues are love, balance, forgiveness, compassion, ego, hope and respect.

Fifth Chakra: Throat Chakra

Located in your neck, the throat chakra vibrates to the note of G and emits the color turquoise. The throat chakra is your center of speech and expression. The throat, neck ears, sinus, thyroid and respiratory systems are associated with the throat chakra. The main issues are communication, healing and creativity.

Sixth Chakra: Third Eye Chakra

Located in the center of your forehead, the third eye chakra vibrates to the note of A and emits the color sapphire-blue. The third eye is your "sixth sense," clairvoyance, imagination, knowing and seeing intuitively. The endocrine, nervous system, awareness and pituitary glands are affected by this chakra. The main issues the third eye chakra governs are intuition, understanding, psychic awareness and focusing on the big picture.

Seventh Chakra: Crown Chakra

Located at the crown of your head, the crown chakra vibrates to the note of B and emits the color purple and/or white. The crown is associated with your central nervous system, head, brain, upper spine and the pineal gland. The crown is your connection to the Divine, wisdom, inspiration and spirituality. The main issues tend to be enlightenment, spiritual understanding and connection to higher power.

Affirmation:

"My thoughts are positive, and I always express myself truthfully and clearly."

The seven stages of chakra connection:

1. Meditation attunes each chakra.

2. The chakra itself opens fully in a receiving and releasing mode.

3. The release of old energy flows out through the center of the chakra.

4. Once the old energy flows outward, the chakra can begin opening fully in a receiving mode.

5. As the Divine energy begins to flow inward, your soul energy can connect with the Divine.

6. Spirit connects your being to the higher Soul Self.

7. Spirit connects your energy to God's Divine energy.

How I can best explain when the divine energy has filled the entire energetic body? This is when love, joy and compassion take the space where the debris of life's energetic junk had previously been stored.

Once you begin a practice of balancing your chakra system, you, too, will feel and see the changes in many ways. The changes that came to me when I first started this practice were subtle at first—a boost in energy, a shift in thought, the release of baggage. Then the tones of healing came from some of the release. When the tones for healing came, I allowed them to flow rather than constrict them with words and trying to make sense of them. Spirit showed me that these tones don't always need our human thought, emotion or sense of exactly what is being healed. What is needed is faith with willingness, partnered with the intent to be healed.

Chakras are energy-awareness centers. They are the revolving doors of creativity and communication between spirit and the world.
~Michael J. Tamura

Healthy Flow

There is deep wisdom within our very flesh, if we can only come to our senses and feel it.

~Elizabeth A. Behnke

Having a basic understanding of the chakra system can help you begin to be more open to a healthy flow. This is just a glimpse—there's much more!

- ❀ Focusing on healing the chakras can bring up emotions.

- ❀ Opening your chakras energizes your body.

- ❀ Opening your crown chakra leads you to your higher self.

- ❀ When all of your chakras are in alignment, you will be able to hear your Inner Goddess clearly.

- ❀ Chakra balancing can heal your mind, body and spirit.

- ❀ Chakra balancing can open your intuitive abilities, allowing your gifts to shine through.

- ❀ Chakra balancing can open your creative centers.

- ❀ Chakra balancing can potentially bring healing to medical issues.

- ❀ Chakra healing can rid your body of toxins.

How Can You Clear Your Chakras?

There are several different and effective methods to help clear your chakras' energy centers. Here are just a few:

Meditation- Try the basic chakra mediation provided on the following page.

Singing Bowls- Singing bowls that are tuned to the specific notes of the chakras can aid in opening and balancing your chakras.

Reiki/Energy/Healer- Learn Reiki or energy healing, or make an appointment with a Reiki master or energy healer. Just be sure to ask beforehand if they are a God-based healer!

Spiritual Medium/Healer- A spiritual medium and healer can "see" where you need to focus your energy and guide you in opening your chakras.

Change of Diet- Changing to a high vibrational diet will help open your chakras.

Music- Music is high vibrational therefore it is uplifting and healing for your chakras.

Basic Chakra Meditation

Affirmation: "I am complete and one with the Divine energy."

❀ Study the chakras list provided.

❀ Have your journal close by.

❀ Set your intention on having the willingness to open your chakras.

❀ Start by getting comfortable. With your spine straight. Allow your breathing cycle to relax you.

❀ Place your hands over your root chakra. Bring your breath slowly down, all the way to your root chakra. Hold the breath with a light pelvic hold. Release this breath with control; in your mind, visualize the chakra opening with a vivid red light. Be one with this red energy for a moment.

❀ Move your hand to your sacral chakra, just below the navel. Allow your breath to come to the sacral chakra while illuminating a radiant orange light. Stay in the orange vibration for a moment before moving to your solar plexus chakra.

❀ As the breath enters the solar plexus chakra, see it unfold into a yellow vibration. Feel this yellow energy opening your solar plexus.

❀ Gently move to your heart chakra and, while doing so, feel your breath filling the area with vibrant green energy. Simply allow the energy to do its own work here.

❀ Move your hands up to your throat chakra. Feel the breath opening the throat with turquoise energy. Feel the chakra opening and spinning.

❀ Move to your third eye chakra. Observe while the third eye opens to a sapphire-blue vibration. Feel this energy gently clearing the third eye chakra.

❀ Place your hands on the crown of your head. See the crown chakra fill with the abundance of white light. Stay in this moment as long as you can. Notice all of the sensations and feelings that are brought to your awareness.

❀ Now ask the Angels to connect your chakras to God's energy. Stay in this energy as long as you feel is needed.

❀ When you are ready, journal the experience(s) you had while completing this exercise.

Action Steps

❀ Do the basic chakra meditation every day for a week.

❀ Compare your journal entries at the end of the week with the entries you wrote at the start of the week. What has changed?

Principle Eight

Healthy, Wealthy and Wise

Once I began a regular practice of chakra balancing, many things shifted in my life. For one, I had a newfound energy. This energy lifted my abilities even more. By removing blocks within the energy system of my body, I also shifted my awareness to seeing a bird's eye view of past events and life in general. This is when Spirit brought forth another vital lesson of wisdom. The lesson was broken into three categories: healthy, wealthy and wise.

Spirit showed me each category works to balance another and that together they make up the wisdom of our true selves. When one is off, the whole balance is off. In other words, your intuition is off.

Wisdom is your intuitive side. It is that gut feeling that speaks to you, the soft voice that speaks out from within when you are in need. This inner wisdom is a loving tone, and each and every one of us has inner wisdom. Learning to tap into it takes just a bit of practice!

Spirit led me to understanding the gift of intuition in a most amusing way. It started with Spirit's message to write a Goddess You course and develop my own Reiki manuals.

I began leading healing sessions and some Reiki classes. I was forcing the work, though. Here's how: rather than let the work come to me with the ease of Spirit's guidance, I began to offer free sessions—free classes on a quickly conceived version of Goddess You boot camp and Reiki level trainings without writing my own manuals, just to get started.

Then Spirit gave me insight on ways to begin, and I followed them, but in other ways, I was forcing it. What follows are some of the valuable lessons I learned from this behavior.

Lesson One: When you give a service away, it is not valued.

By giving away free sessions and classes, I learned that the people who received them did not value the service. Forcing the work was not as fulfilling for me or for the other person.

Valuing others' time frame for healing or learning became a new focus. That opened the pathway for Spirit to bring forward those individuals who were ready and did need my tone.

I was shown the sign: Let go and let God. Amen to that!

Lesson Two: Slow down and let the flow of the message have a chance to marinate into your life with its new energy.

This was a tough one, as my energy moves very quickly. I found patience with breathing techniques, which helped me to be in a calmer energy groove, yet remain high vibrational.

I also found that the messages Spirit was giving me were clearer within that calmer groove. "Now ease up and slow down" was the tone from Spirit!

Lesson Three: Angels don't lie, so listen up!

Messages bring forth many amazing changes. The messages are always for our highest and best good. It is our free will to follow the guidance or avoid it. Avoidance then is our barrier that keeps us from the outcome we desire. So why do we choose to ignore the messages? Well, that is why you are here- so you can discover your blocks, heal your fears and live in soul alignment. I have learned, after avoiding several repeat messages, that I was going to remain in the same perpetual state unless I shifted the view and followed the guidance.

Journal Prompt:

Are you noticing the tone

of guidance Spirit

is sending you?

You don't have to be a medium for guidance to come to you. Your loved ones from the other side can send you loving messages through signs and symbols that resonate with you. Being open-minded and clear in your energy and welcoming to the signs are the ways you invite the signs in. Similarly, Spirit can nudge you in a loving way to help you on your path. Are you open to receive? "Nancy Drew it" all the details in your journal.

Spirit says: "If you build it, they will come." Yes, indeed, Spirit can be a bit sarcastic, too!

So the time and energy wasted on forcing work kept me in a perpetual state of repeating behavior that was not at all healthy, wealthy or wise. Slowing down, taking time off to write the coursework, reflect and groove in the intuitive energy and messages given—are what shifted the energetic flow and brought forward the work in a clearer view.

Clients then began to come on their own. The spiritual energy coming from the writing was beyond what my once-limited thoughts could see. By slowing my energy down in a healthy way, I made room for this new way of living. Now instead of forcing or manipulating energy, I allow. Trust me when I tell you the work is by far more fulfilling for my clients and myself.

Journal Prompt:

What are you

forcing in your life?

Let's Break It Down

Healthy

🌼 Your choices matter. Careful choices are a must for your personal well-be-ing. Slow down, breathe in and let the choice resonate from within your soul.

Wealthy

🌼 Forcing work or staying in a job that does not resonate with you will leave you depleted and unhealthy.

🌼 A rich man is a man who loves what he does.

🌼 Healthy wealth comes from following the wisdom of your soul.

Wise

🌼 Being in alignment with your Soul Self allows your inner guidance sys-tem to work. A wise choice comes from following your intuitive voice.

Healthy, Wealthy and Wise

Diseases of the soul are more dangerous and more numerous than those of the body. ~Cicero

Your Inner Goddess knows what your body needs to function at its highest vibrational rate. Listening to that inner wisdom is never easy. Most people block it out or practice self-sabotage. You do have a deep understanding of what is good and what is not good for you. The goal is to align this knowledge with your Goddess Soul Self. In doing so, you become in tune with your soul's guidance and follow through on the path for your highest and best good. This wisdom opens your passageway in many ways:

HEALTH

❀ It guides you to eat the foods best for body, mind and soul.

WEALTH

❀ It guides you into a field of work where you can use your unique talents, skill sets and gifts.

WISDOM

❀ It aids you in aligning your thoughts and actions with your Goddess Soul Self.

Moving through Grief

Grief: noun; deep sorrow, especially caused by someone's death:

Grief as I have been shown by Spirit is energetic. Which means it can move in and out of both your physical body and your energetic body, otherwise known as your aura. Grief can become a block and keep you from moving in a forward direction. Forward is where love and the Divine can be seen and felt. Fear, aka Shmego is the complete opposite of love and forward Divine direction.

When grief comes into your life it can take on the tone and energy of fear or of love. This is the how and the why that grief will flow either in a healthy or unhealthy way.

A healthy flow is when you are able to express your sorrow through forms of release, such as crying, journaling, talking it out or prayer.

An unhealthy flow is when you shut down and hold the sorrow and pain within your body. Fear brings your thoughts to a negative pattern. Guilt, anger, bitterness, judgment or attachment to how or why the grief came into your life becomes your main focus. The outcome then is that the fear blocks the love from allowing your grief to flow.

Intuition can serve you during the grief process. Allowing you to intuitively connect with your grief and show you how you can allow the pain to serve you rather than to hurt you. This will lead you to instinctively know what your body needs to move through the grief.

Let me explain how grief is a lesson that can teach and guide you by sharing one clients grief story.

In 2014, my friend Pat's husband, Tim, passed away after being diagnosed with cancer just a few months before. One day after his death, I stopped by Pat's office to drop something off to her, and Tim came through to me. He showed me a sun porch. He was very direct with his tone as he showed me construction and more importantly decorating.

I slowly turned to Pat. "Are you doing work on your sun porch?"

She looked at me funny and said, "Yes, how do you know?"

"Well," I said, "Tim is showing me this, and he is happy you are finishing what he started."

Tim let me know he liked her choices. Pat's eyes filled with tears. She was overjoyed that he came through and that he liked what she was choosing to do differently from the original plan. As I left the office, I was grateful that I was able to ease some of her pain. I had no idea it would be the first of many times Tim had an important messages for me to relay to her. Over the course of the past few years, Pat has become not only a friend and colleague but also a client.

The move to become a client came on a cold fall night.

We were all alone at the start of a meeting. I took one look at her and instantly knew why we were the only two people who had arrived early. Tim! We went into a small office where I could deliver Tim's many messages. He had been showing me how grief was affecting her health and well-being by becoming stuck within her chest area. Tim showed me that Pat was closed off and staying in the pain and sorrow of his passing.

He also spoke of his beloved cats and how it would be okay for Pat to let a couple of them move on to new homes in order to help her feel less burdened by their care. Tim also showed me, that he had a passion in life for sheltering stray cats and that Pat had always supported his passion.

Pat had a hard time accepting the message Tim was sending her. She argued that she too had a passion for the cats they together had saved, and did not want to find them new homes.

It was an emotional reading but one that lifted her spirits a bit, and aided in lessening some of the grief that was overwhelming her.

On another occasion, we had an emotional session that came after a tragic event happened at her home. It started with a text that I received from a mutual friend. This friend was reaching out to me about Pat, saying she thought it would be a good idea if I could contact her asap! I knew from the text that something big was up. I called Pat and set up a session for later that day. During the session Pat explained to me that upon coming home from work the day before she had found her garden a mess with broken flowers lying about, and a stray dog in her yard. While observing the destruction, feeling shocked and confused about what had happened she came upon one of her beloved twin cats lying on the ground. Hearing Pat's distraught whimpers, a neighbor came to her aid just as the stray dog ran off leaving the aftermath of its devastating visit. Her neighbor confirmed Pat's worst fear that the cat was indeed lifeless. Upon entering her home Pat discovered that the other twin cat was no where to be found. To add to her misfortune she later found the missing twin cat, who had passed away as well.

After completing her explanation to me, Pat was understandably shaken and weak

from the grief. The session connected her to calmer energy and messages from her husband. Both Tim, and the twin cats came through.

We also spoke about the messages in the earlier reading with Tim. Tim had been guiding her in order to heal her grief. And in doing so he was showing her that by releasing some the of cats that he had brought home, it would allow love to begin to flow again. His guidance was trying to help Pat learn one of her life lessons and open her intuition. He also wanted her to know that the cats were going to leave her whether she wanted them to leave or not. Grief had shaken her from her calm point more than once in her life. And so grief was repeating the pattern so she could learn and grow closer to the Divine instead of further away.

Pat has since been able to allow the grief to flow with the Divine. Finding peace and joy in the messages and reconnecting to her intuition. Pat is now opening her life in new adventurous ways. Choosing to live forward instead of with fear. She has stepped outside her comfort zone and allowed love to lead her in a bright new direction.

Her journey, though not an easy one, but one many can relate to, is an opportunity where a great lesson can be learned for each of us. That the truth that flows through our intuition can be the guide to learn and grow. That lessons are not easy, but they can be rewarding if we can see the love within them. Spirit has shown me that souls work together to assist each other in learning our life lessons and growing closer to the Divine. And that the Divine does not punish because God is love.

Healthy

A healthy outside starts from the inside. ~Robert Urich

Many layers contribute to meeting your optimal health. Listed below are just a few of the basics.

Understanding that foods hold vibration can help you to see that what you choose to eat truly affects your mind, body and spirit. Every single person has a different vibrational rate. Listening to the vibration of food can help you connect with the best food choices for you.

Here's a quick trick for you: a good way to know how food vibrates is to understand that when it is in its purest state, it vibrates the highest. For example, fresh vegetables (just picked) are at the peak of their energy vibration. When you cook them, they lose some of their vibration, and when you freeze them, they lose even more. Most frozen foods hold a very low vibration and are lower in nutrients. When foods are processed, their energy is broken down, and this changes the food's original nutritional composition. An example of a high vibrational food is maple syrup, but only in its purest state. When it is cooked down to make sugar, it loses the high vibration, and its health value diminishes. Meat is a medium-vibration food. The truth is that some people need to consume meat to be healthy, while others do not. We must learn to really hear what our body needs.

Juicing is a great source of a high vibrational food. It is a great way to quickly raise your energy levels. Juicing is also very healing for the body.

Action Steps

✿ Set your intention on connecting with your energy.

✿ Take a moment to hear your body's vibrational rate. You might ask, "How the heck do I do that?" Well, start by sitting upright in a chair, plant your feet firmly on the ground, close your eyes and begin doing cycle breathing, which is breath work in which you pay attention to the full cycle of inhaling and exhaling.

✿ While cycle breathing, place your hands over your heart. Sit in this moment and come into your body. Feel your heart beating and imagine your blood flowing.

✿ Listen to your breath. Get lost in calming yourself down. Feel the rise and fall of your chest. Sit as long as you need.

✿ Journal your findings.

Wealthy

Acknowledging the good that you already have in your life is the foundation for all abundance.

~Eckhart Tolle

Wealth is another form of health. Wealth is not measured only by the accumulation of money. Wealth is measured by your life relationships, your accomplishments, moments of joy and wise use of your gifts. All these aspects bring you wealth.

Monetary items are not wealth. Although they are nice to have, you must consider the price you pay for them and how much they deplete your energy. Items can deplete your energy when they become a burden. They can become an addiction, or they can be dormant. To create new wealth in your life, you must look at what energies are holding you back.

Here is just a little something to think about: to live in alignment with your healthy, wealthy and wise Inner Goddess, you may have to change your old ways to create the healthy, new you.

Get your Inner Goddess groove on and lighten your load! Move that energy with the intent of inviting healthy wealth into your life. A great place to begin is by doing space clearing. This allows the new and improved energy to enter your living space.

Action Steps

❀ Grab your journal!

❀ Ask yourself these questions:

❀ What is holding me back?

❀ What things are carrying the heaviest energy in my life at the present time?

❀ Can I let these things go?

❀ What type of wealth am I attracting?

❀ What type of wealth do I want to attract?

❀ What actions do I have to take in order to change my old ways?

Wise

Knowledge is learning without a limit. ~Lailah Gifty Akita

Living in alignment with your Inner Goddess is what makes you wise. When you choose to be connected to a higher power and flow in that unconditional love energy, well, my friend, that is when the "aha" moment happens!

Go through your cabinets and your refrigerator. Remove the items that don't align with your body. Hold them in your hands. Feel the vibration before you pack them up to send them off to a needy family or your local food pantry.

Removing the processed foods from your stock will help you get over the temptation to indulge.

This is the perfect time for my favorite field trip: the farmers market!

The next time you go to your local farmers market or supermarket, really take your time in the produce section. Feel the vibration from the fresh fruit and vegetables. Let your eyes lead you to certain items.

Once home, do a little experiment of holding a fresh item and a frozen item in each hand; compare the difference you feel.

Journal Prompt:

Record your findings!

Principle Nine

Keep Calm

Grooving in the flow of my inner wisdom led me down yet another insightful path. Another door opened. This door had many locks and bolts on it. Some of the keys or combinations had been lost within the storms of my life. The storms were everyday happenings and events that would suck up my energy. Rather than being able to navigate through an event with a sense of calm, I was getting lost and becoming the stormy energy. This is when Spirit guided me to understand the important lesson of keeping calm.

As always, the message from Spirit came to me at a time it was most needed. Having a large family means having lots of events. Events for me run yearly and are always combined together in what I call the "big threes" and the "little threes," meaning that when three major events are happening, three smaller events are going on at the same time.

The three events have been one of my life lessons. Learning how to properly navigate through them without getting my crazy on has been a serious challenge.

Let me give you examples of my experience with the big threes and the little threes.

Journal Prompt:

Reflect on your life now and notice from another view how you move through it. Event to event? Career to career? Keeping up a false persona? Whirling in and out of friendships? Be open and add no judgments to your findings. Jot them down in **Goddess You Journal.**

1985

Big Threes

- My wedding
- The birth of our first child
- My hubby went to rehab

Little Threes

- A car accident
- I left beauty school
- I moved back in with my parents

1996

Big Threes

- The birth of our fourth child
- The purchase of my husband's business
- My grandfather passed away

Little Threes

- Clearing out my grandfather's house
- We moved to a new home
- We took in our first foster child

2011

Big Threes

- Our daughter married
- Our son married
- Our first grandchild was born

Little Threes

- I closed my shoe store
- My son-in-law went to Afghanistan
- Our son graduated highschool

You get the picture. These events grouped together in time as well, and they challenged me to stay calm. I will be the first to admit I have not always been able to keep the calm as my main focus. I would instead focus on the energy surrounding the event, and that energy would then dictate how I would act and react. That's a whole bunch of crazy!

Spirit taught me to go above the event or situation, to use a bird's eye view. Along with the other principles and tools, I could raise my vision out of the event's energy to see where my energy would best be used and at the same time keep my energy within my being. Over time, with practice, I was able to move my view so I could see the event from the side as well. This offered me the steadiness that I needed to navigate through it while knowing the best actions to take.

Try using the bird's eye view to deepen your understanding of how you move through stressful times. See if you can disconnect from ego to better understand yourself and navigate through challenging times on a higher vibration.

Keep Calm and Carry the Flock On

Speak when you're angry and you'll make the best speech you'll ever regret! ~Laurence J. Peter

Calm is your bliss state. When you are calm, life flows so sweetly.

When you are "crazy," life brings you more crazy!

Rest is essential to calm your body. While in a restful state, you allow your Inner Goddess to shine through with ease.

Panic leads to the "freak state of mind."

Keeping cool during difficult and stressful times is not an easy task for most people. You tend to allow the drama of the situation, or Shmego's voice to take control. It is at that crucial point when drama or ego surface and start to overwhelm you when you need to get your calm on, and fast! It may be hard to recognize at first, but as soon as you notice, use your tools to get your calm on. You can and will pick yourself up, dust yourself off and carry the flock on.

There should be a warning sign flashing in large red letters and an obnoxious beeping sound: "You have now entered the freak zone!"

Truth be told, swearing is a form of release. It's a way to make a strong, firm point. (I may have made that up.) Plus, I like to swear sometimes. (Truth!)

Get Your Calm On

Real difficulties can be overcome: It is only the imaginary ones that are unconquerable.

~Theodore N. Vail

Letting go of the common thought of how things could have gone in a situation will help you to carry on.

Remind yourself: compassion for all! In every situation, stand in the light and find the compassion.

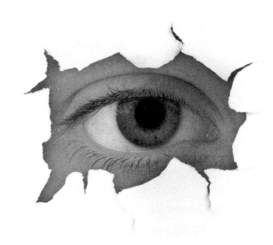

Cycle breathing relaxes and releases. As a bonus for some people, it lowers blood pressure.

Alcohol and drug use increase our freak factor, so keep them to a bare minimum, especially during stressful times.

Healthy food choices will keep you in harmony with your Inner Goddess. Grab a green juice and feel the flow of calm take over.

Exercise, my friend, because it helps release stress hormones. Get your heart pumping to feel that flow of calm.

Additionally, journaling is a great way to release the crazy you feel.

Love looks forward,
hate looks back,
anxiety has
eyes all over its head.
~Mignon McLaughlin

Cry it out. Get a good old cry out and release through your tears. It will help calm your inner "she beast," as I call her.

Get your crazy out by yelling. Go to a quiet zone and have a good old screaming match all by yourself. Swear, stomp your feet, jump up and down or choose your own way to let it out. Try doing it in the car when you are all alone. It is so much fun to really let loose.

Flocking Homework

Continuous effort—not strength or intelligence—is the key to unlocking our potential.

~Winston S. Churchill

❀ Grab your journal!

❀ Start your cycle breathing. Relax, and when you are ready . . .

❀ Take a little time travel. Remember a time when you really lost your calm. Take some time to see yourself at the moment in time. Write down the following:

- o Where were you?

- o How did you feel?

- o What do you notice most about that moment?

- o Can you feel your body at that time? What does it feel like?

- o Can you:

    • Smell anything?

    • Feel anything?

    • Hear anything?

    • See anything?

Now notice:

❀ What is different about you now?

❀ How do you keep your calm now?

❀ If you lose your calm, what action steps would you take to calm yourself?

❀ How have you grown and changed from then to now?

This exercise will help you to see your progress. Whether you have just started your journey to tune in with your Inner Goddess or you are living in alignment with her every day, you can look back and see your words on paper, feel your growth in your words and actions, and accept the changed woman you are today.

Rock on, my friend, rock on!!

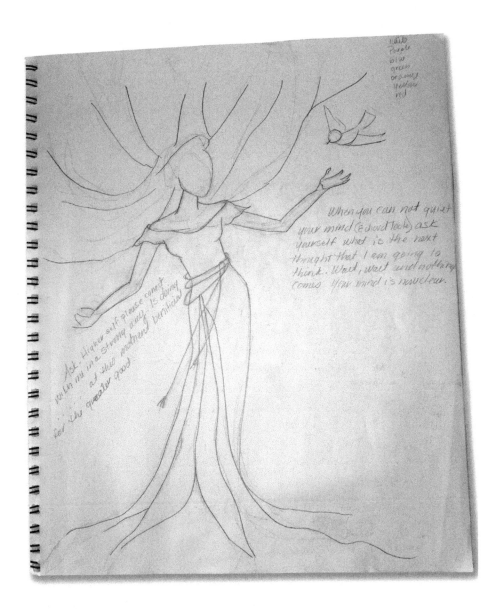

White
Purple
blue
green
orange
yellow
red

When you can not quiet your mind (e chord Toole) ask yourself what is the next thought that I am going to think. Wait, wait and nothing comes. Your mind is nowhere.

Ask Higher self please connect with me in a strong way. Is doing at this moment beneficial for the greater good.

129

Principle Ten

Balance

The lesson of balance came in soon after the principle of keeping calm. Spirit showed me that balance and keeping calm go hand in hand. You can't have one without the other. Balance can be tricky to achieve, especially for those of us who are empaths and highly vibrational.

Although the lesson of keeping calm worked like a charm when I utilized it, I have since, at times, fallen off the pathway and gone into the crazy energy. The only difference is that I can recognize the craziness much quicker and plug back into Spirit's guidance to heal or calm the crazy with confidence and ease.

The tools Spirit has guided me to use help bring the balance needed to achieve the calm. Or, sometimes it is vice versa: I find calm, and that brings the balance back.

Which comes first—the calm or the balance? It's kind of like the chicken or the egg: you can't have one without the other. So balance leads to calm, but to get balance, you need to be calm.

You get the idea: the twelve Goddess you principles are equally important.

The first step in regaining balance is, of course, acknowledgment. Once you can see the crazy, you can heal it. Meditation, prayer and breath

work are the first go-tos. They are the fastest and easiest ways to balance yourself. And the bonus is that you can do them anywhere and anytime.

Let me share with you how I recently used these tools in my life.

Not long ago we had our usual big threes/little threes happening. While I was attending to one of the events, I began to lose balance and a sense of calm. Crazy was coming, and I knew I had to act quickly.

The lowdown? My hubby, who had just had surgery, was asking to go to the emergency room at the same time that our ninety-five-year-old Nana was getting ready to pass. We had been sitting by her side since 3:00 a.m. at the nursing home. Earlier that morning, about 1:00 a.m., our son and his wife had welcomed in the birth of their first baby and our third granddaughter. Exciting and amazing—our sweet Hadley came a week early! Thankfully, we had been able to leave Nana in the care of other family members during the day so we could go meet our sweet grand baby.

But with my husband in pain now, crazy was knocking.

At about 8:00 p.m. I was at the emergency room with him while trying to arrange for my daughter to relieve me so I could go back to sit with Nana. I knew that I could not contain the emotional energy. Tears began to flow. My husband felt terrible that I was crying, but I assured him that it was not him. "This is my way to stay balanced," I told him. Fortunately, he gets me and my connection to Spirit. We chatted a bit about what the Angels were saying about the day when the ER doctor announced that he couldn't help my husband at this hospital. "You will have to go to back to the hospital where you had the surgery," he said.

"What?" I asked. Then I stopped and noticed. I thought to myself: this is where the crazy would normally come in. I immediately put into practice the action steps to regain balance. I started with a prayer and invited the Angels to assist me. At the same time I began with cycle breathing to connect and reestablish my balance. I used the tool of the bird's eye view to see the current event from its' highest vibration. This allowed me to direct my focus to see what was needed to keep the energy in a calm state. The first thing I could see was the need to separate each energetic event. By doing this, I could function on the one energetic event that needed my attention at that moment. I asked the Angels for their help while using mental imagery to disconnect each energy from the other. The events then began to separate. Now I could release the built-up energy from within my body, and I could let the crazy go. The breath brought another wave of tears, which served as the release pathway for the crazy energy to leave my body. Each breath also opened each energy center, focusing on the ones in my feet and in the hip area. Being present in the moment was now sustainable.

Spirit has shown me the importance of energy having a point of release. That buildup of crazy, unbalanced energy is what leads to confusion, anxiety, depression, muscle aches and tight joints. Holding things together, so to speak, is temporary. For each and every action, there is a reaction. Not allowing a reaction and containing it, surprisingly, is the path to being out of balance.

Back to the story:

As tears flowed, I spoke in a calm tone to the doctor. "The two hospitals are affiliated, and the surgeon sees patients here as well as at the other hospital. Honestly, I just cannot go that far away." I gave him the view of our day thus far in a calm rational tone. (So un-like the old me! :))

And guess what—it was totally effective! The ER doctor agreed with me and changed his tone. He decided to run some tests. So then I could go on with my plan to get back to Nana. I was honored to be by her side as she crossed over. My hubby got the antibiotics he needed, and all was as calm as it could be.

So, thanks to my Angels, and the twelve principles, yet again!

Balancing Business

Quiet the mind, and the soul will speak. ~Ma Jaya Sati Bhagavati

Feeling out of sorts? Losing your mind? Have a feeling that the onset of crazy has hit and is coming your way? Does everything seem to happen too fast? Feel like you can't get out of your own way? Are you fighting with loved ones? Are feelings of anger, frustration or anxiety frequently creeping into your life? These are just a few of the emotions you might feel when you are off balance.

You have to remember that you are human, and it is perfectly normal to lose your balance. The key is to have the tools accessible to pick yourself up, dust off the mess and move back to your balanced way of being.

The first order of the "balancing business" is to recognize and admit to yourself that you might be off your rocker. Just kidding! What I meant to say is: you're off balance. It is now that you can start the process. Get back in touch with equalizing your state of mind.

One of the quickest ways to re-sync with your Inner Goddess is (I bet you'll never guess) meditation!

Yes, yes! I know it can seem annoying to keep hearing about meditation. I felt the same exact way, but what I have finally learned, is that when I let go of all that is around me and begin that cycle breathing, a sense of calm and serenity sets back in quickly and effortlessly.

Over the years of not listening to Spirit's voice, I definitely spent way too much time searching for different ways to get my balance back. While some things I stumbled upon worked just fine, they seemed to have a short lifespan, and they did not work as quickly as meditation.

Finding Your Balance

You yourself, as much as anybody in the entire universe, deserve your love and affection.

~Buddha

Balance is the stability of your mind or feelings. Managing your mind and your feelings are the way to some kind of peace and personal balance.

Finding balance in a busy life is not always easy, especially when you are not living in alignment with your Inner Goddess and the Divine connection to God, a.k.a., a higher power. It is through your connection to God that you can find balance in your everyday life, and peace and comfort in times of need. It is essential throughout your journey of unleashing your Inner Goddess to allow love in from

Inner peace is the key: if you have inner peace, external problems do not affect your deep sense of peace and tranquility…. Without this inner peace, no matter how comfortable your life is materially, you may still be worried, disturbed or unhappy because of circumstances.
~Dalai Lama XIV

a higher power. This is when balance will become your reality.

To achieve balance in your life, you must also have faith and love working as a team to form peace.

Peace is freedom from disturbance—quiet and tranquil . Peace is your balance. Faith and love are your passageways to achieving the balanced life for which you are searching.

Gregory Peck's view on faith is, "Faith gives you an inner strength, a sense of balance and perspective in life."

Marianne Williamson says, "Everything we do is infused with the energy with which we do it. If we're frantic, life will be frantic. If we're peaceful, life will be peaceful. And so our goal in any situation becomes inner peace."

Finding your balance requires a conscious effort and clear intent. Your Inner Goddess is a guiding light to the state of balance.

Keys for Unlocking Your Balance

Be faithful in small things because it is in them that your strength lies … -Mother Teresa

- ❀ **Faith**
- ❀ **Intention**
- ❀ **Calm**
- ❀ **Health**
- ❀ **Love**
- ❀ **Letting Go**
- ❀ **Rest**
- ❀ **Relaxation**
- ❀ **Meditation**
- ❀ **Gratitude**
- ❀ **Prayer**
- ❀ **Compassion**

Balancing Homework

Be love, feel love, live love.

For this exercise, you are going to be a special assignment detective. So, grab your journal and carry these detective tools with you on your journey.

Your assignment: people-watch.

❀ Listen to the tone in which people speak.

❀ Notice how their body language speaks for them.

❀ Write down all of your impressions (not judgments).

❀ When you lose your balance, jot down:

     o   How do you feel?

     o   How do you stand?

     o   How do you sound?

     o   What do you feel?

Action Steps

❀ Do a chakra balancing meditation to regain your balance.

❀ See yourself and others through your heart center. Remember, compassion for all.

❀ Be love, feel love, live love!

❀ Connect to God, or your higher power. Opening up your faith restores balance.

❀ Gratitude is a must-have.

❀ Be calm.

❀ What other impressions do you notice?

❀ Compare your findings of people-watching with the impressions of yourself.

❀ Do you notice anything familiar in the way they react?

❀ What does your body language say about you?

❀ Are you standing tall? Are you standing with purpose?

Principle Eleven

Mind Body Spirit

You are made up of these three little gems—the mind, the body and the soul. Each one contains a unique energy.

Spirit has taught me the importance of knowing and understanding the energy of each one separately. I have learned to utilize the mind energy along with the body energy to create a strong spiritual connection.

Our souls, or spirits, live within each of us. Many believe the chest cavity is the seat of the soul. The soul or Spirit Self is infinite—it continues on and on. The Soul Self, when you are connected to it, can open you to the how, why and what of life—the reason you are here.

Although the soul resides in the body, that does not mean you are always flowing together in unison with your Soul Self. Your body energy and mind energy can become separated from your soul. Separation is energetic: the energy from the soul truth cannot flow freely through your body and mind, when fragmented. That is how you lose your way on your life path. Confusion, depression, bad choices, argumentativeness, egotistical statements, resentment, blaming others—these are some of the signs that you are not in communion with the mind, body, soul connection.

Spirit guided me to connect each vibrational energy of the mind, body and soul, and that brought me a sense of calm and well-being that I had not known before. Flowing in this groove invited in the view of how the work I was doing and going to do would shift not only my energy and life, but also that of others whose energy would cross my path. I learned that not only do I guide and help clients, I receive in return, their offer of lessons and deepening of my faith. The work lifts low vibrations to higher, healthy vibrations.

For a long time I was lost in the idea that enlightenment was out of my reach. Enlightenment, I have learned through Spirit's teachings, is a state of mind. You can access this state by your intentions and a willingness to be in a higher vibration.

Enlightenment is what comes to you when you are able to shed the ego mind. Following the twelve principles has helped me to be in communion with Spirit. And it can help you to reach your personal goal of spiritual enlightenment as well.

You can attain different levels of clarity each time you practice the Goddess principles. Pretty cool, right?

Let's Break It Down

Mind energy comes from your thoughts. Clear thoughts, focus and intention come from being mindful.

Meditation and breath work are your tools to have a high vibrational mind energy center. Knowing the tone of ego helps to keep the mind clear of cluttered energy.

Body energy comes from what you put into your body.

From food to stress, what you are swallowing affects your body's vibration.

To maintain your body's healthy vibration, know what foods serve you, know how to manage stress, exercise and practice meditation.

Spirit or soul energy comes from your faith and spiritual connection.

A daily practice of prayer and meditation, combined with faith, are your tools for grooving in the high vibration of Spirit.

I have struggled with the normal routine of life, trying to

fit in and conform to others' views of who and what I am or should be. This, of course, feels yucky and unfulfilling. Others' thoughts of you are just that—their thoughts. Being authentically you takes courage. Courage, for me, came from following the Goddess you principles while embracing my Soul Self. Though it is not always easy to get out of my own way at times, Spirit's loving nudge serves as a reminder that it does matter that you and I live within the energy of the twelve Goddess principles.

Mind, Body, Spirit

All is connected... no one thing can change by itself. ~Paul Hawken

For you to stay connected to your Inner Goddess, you must have a mind, body and spirit connection, and that means your mind and body must be functioning on a high vibrational level and must be open to the Divine. When this alignment happens, you will achieve a strong connection with Spirit.

Your connection between your mind, your body and your spirit will have you moving and grooving with your Inner Goddess.

Reflecting on what you have experienced so far in this book, you should see that you have opened yourself up to the amazing love and guidance that is always within your reach. You started with mind lessons, learning about ego thoughts versus love thoughts. You slowed down your thoughts through cycle breathing. Then, you moved on to learning how to care for your body, how healthy food choices and exercise can raise your vibration. From there, you learned about chakra balancing—the key to releasing old energy. Through all of the lessons, the common thread has been journaling and meditation combined with consistently setting your intention. And now you are moving on to the conclusion of the most amazing journey your Inner Goddess will take: the Spirit connection.

Divine connection is the "aha" moment for which you should always strive. Without it, honestly, you will stay the same. With it, you will grow and blossom beyond your own expectations. For what the Divine will lead you to will simply amaze you!

Divine

Of, from, or like God or a god; devoted to God; sacred.

Connection

The connection to the Divine opens your intuition and insights. Divine connection in and of itself is not a religion. You will need faith in God or a higher power of your choice.

Faith

Belief that is not based on proof. Know that to have faith, you must have love. Love is the constant in everything. Love never fails. It is your choices that fail, not love. Hopes and dreams can change, but the love remains. Your love for God, love of self, love of others should always be present. Relationships can change; sometimes it seems they take a turn for the worse. But, as you now know, if you see the other person through compassion and love, you can forgive. And that, my friend, is the love you thought you lost. It is how you choose to be that matters. Love is the connection to the Divine. Changing your thoughts to love thoughts, seeing others through the eyes of love, forgiving through faith and love are all your "tools" that can change every situation, open your gifts and allow you to become one with your Inner Goddess.

With Divine connection:

❀ Intuition gets stronger.

❀ Your gifts are present and open to the world around you.

❀ Relationships improve.

❀ New doorways open for you.

❀ Your life purpose can be seen and felt.

Through these action steps you can really open the gates to your own amazing intuition.

When you let go of all ego thoughts and hear your true Inner Goddess, everything comes together. Your Divine connection is then complete. Thus it is known as the mind-body-spirit connection.

Homework

The history of your happiness is the history of your feeling connected.
~Vironika Tugaleva

Get your Inner Goddess groove on!

Start your day with the intent of being connected to the Divine. Say a prayer, ask to be open and connected to Divine love throughout your day. Then do a short meditation and concentrate on opening your chakras, especially your third eye chakra.

Remember your third eye chakra is where you receive information. You will be able to feel your intuition in your body. The strongest place to access this feeling is in your solar plexus chakra—or as most people refer to it, their gut.

Have your journal ready.

With every action you take today, flow through it as your intuitive self. Hear the tone of your Inner Goddess streaming through your thoughts. Her tone will be loving and kind, so there is no mistaking her with Shmego (who is fear-based).

Start with breakfast. Allow two choices of food; put your hand on your chest to feel your body's rhythm and ask what would best serve your mind, body and soul today. Do this for each meal. Then follow the action steps.

Do this exercise each day this week.

Live each day with purpose and connection.

Action Steps

❋ Cycle-breathe to start your day.

  Journal about :

  • What is the first thing you felt?

  • Was it in a loving tone?

  • How did it feel?

❋ Use this form of connection throughout your day when you face different choices. Journal about your connections and your findings.

Principle Twelve

Intuitive, Gifted You

Each principle leads you to a deeper connection to your intuition. To follow your Divine path, you will need to align with your Soul-Self. Grooving in your higher intuition will bring forward your Divine gifts.

Your Divine gifts are unique to you. Although we may have similar gifts, it is important to understand that the uniqueness of your gifts, along with how you use them, is key to living in alignment with your Soul Self.

Along the journey of following the principles and awakening to my gifts, I was taught how to recognize not only my personal gifts but also the gifts of others. This insight was helpful in teaching me the depth of how to remain in my own energy and the energy of the gift.

Let me explain: Spirit then taught me about the different types of gifts and how the energy of each one can get confused or tangled up. The principles helped to reconnect my body, mind and soul with the gifts. They helped me bring forward that confused energy so that I could untangle it. Meditation cleared the energetic channels to the gifts. This brought a calmness, along with a clear understanding of how each of the gifts can be used. The questions of how and why they should be used became clearer once I learned how to balance each gift's energy.

Understanding your Gifts

Understanding your gifts is an important part of uncovering who you are. Each gift is broken down by common traits of energy. You may notice you have only some of the traits within a gift, which is absolutely normal. You can then use that energy to enhance your stronger gifts. You also can grow that gift with a steady practice of meditation and prayer.

Clairs, as they are widely referred to, are the pathways used to connect and transmit Spirit's messages.

Clairvoyance

The ability to see Spirit, to see in the mind's eye. Clairvoyants can see clearly in their mind's eye or as if Spirit is standing right in front of them.

Clairaudience

The ability to hear the voice of Spirit. With the gift of clairaudience, one can clearly hear words, songs or tones of Spirit.

Clairsentience

The ability to know Spirit's message through a feeling or in your physical body.

Clairalience

The ability to smell Spirit's message. The ability to clearly smell the message from Spirit.

Clairgustance

The ability to taste Spirit's message.

Clairenunuciate

The ability to communicate with Spirit.

Claircognizance

The ability of clear knowing.

Intuition

A gut feeling or clear knowing.

Understanding your intuition is crucial to bringing all of your gifts together. Everyone is intuitive, but not everyone uses or trusts his or her intuition. God has blessed us with this inner guidance system that can lead, support and guide us through life.

The best course of action to understanding your gifts is understanding who you are. Your journey through the twelve Goddess you principles is the key to a clear view and better understanding of that beautiful you. Meditation combined with journaling offers you a place to release and relish the tones of the journey.

Honoring your feelings without the tone of ego is how you can see the real you.

Shining your light outward to others is how you honor and grow your gifts.

The Gift of Empath

Also Known as Clairsentience

The ability to feel another's pain, suffering, illness and energy. An empath can take on the energy of others as if it is literally their own.

Having the gift of being an empath can be tricky. It can take time and dedication to understand what energy belongs to you and what energy belongs to another. And after years, being unaware of having taken on energy that was not your own, it is possible that you may have damaged your own being with the fear and energy you unknowingly took on from others. Those fears and that energy become woven into your energy centers, manifesting physically.

"Wait, did you just say physical manifestation?" you may ask. Yes, your mind actually believes it is ill, so you become ill. You are what you think, and your thoughts become reality. This is why it is so important for an empath to become familiar with their own being.

As you can begin to understand there are many downsides to living a life as an empath, but there are also amazing benefits.

Here are a few of the advantages of being an empath: being able to help others just by knowing, being able to feel love on a soul level, being able to tap into the inner guidance of the knowing and being able to see others on a soul level.

A key that I have found for my health and wellness is purification with Divine connection. The tools that have helped me to attain this purification are: prayer, meditation, clear intent, knowing my energy and self love, these tools are as important to my well-being as insulin is to a diabetic. Without them, I can go into energetic overload that can shock my energy system and cause an energetic shutdown.

Tools to Grooving in Your Intuitive Soul Self

Follow the twelve Goddess You principles:

❀ clear and heal the energy that blocks you from connecting to your intuition.

Put your faith in the guidance:

❀ faith opens your view with your connection to the Divine. It deepens the level of intuition.

Open up to your creativity:

❀ creative energy opens the intuitive flow.

Move with clear intention:

❀ intention sets the tone and leads to your outcome.

Use the knowledge of Spirit's lessons:

❀ this will lead you on the pathway for living in soul alignment, understanding who you are and knowing your soul purpose.

You, too, might be an empath

When you balance what is yours you can then understand your life and the work your soul is here to do. The blessing of this gift is in helping others.

Empath out of control a.k.a out of alignment

- ✿ Withdrawn
- ✿ Depressed
- ✿ Angry
- ✿ Overindulgent/borderline addict
- ✿ Feeling Flu-like all the time
- ✿ Over/under sympathetic
- ✿ Drama magnet
- ✿ Hyper
- ✿ Anxious

Before I understood that I was an empath I was confused about what was going on in my body. I looked for answers in many places, and one of them was traditional medicine. Doctors had diagnosed me with a variety of afflictions based solely on symptoms I was feeling. I have since come to find out that none of them were actually my illness. Instead, they were illnesses of people with whom I was close or with whom I came into contact. Without my survival tools, these illnesses could have grown into full-blown serious conditions. No, thank you!

Journal Prompt:

Is your soul work becoming more in focus? What does it look like and feel like?

Meditation: Discovering your Gifts

Have The *Goddess You Journal* nearby.

Start with cycle breathing. Allow your body to let go and just be in the moment. With each breath in, feel your muscles relaxing and releasing.

Feel your legs letting go, your arms letting go, your back relaxing. Just let all the tension escape your body. The breath is guiding you.

Allow your mind to be open and clear. As you take in the next breath, see yourself sitting on the most amazing beach you could ever imagine.

As the wave of the ocean rolls up, let your whole body just melt into the sound and motion while allowing each new wave to bring you more and more relaxation.

Smell the air. Feel the ocean mist and the rays of the sun warming your skin.

As you sit on this beach, notice the clouds starting to take shape into the form of an Angel, and just as the moment flashes, this angel-form is standing right in front of you.

You now know you are safe and loved. The Angel is a symbol of pure love, so you can feel and sense the love

surrounding and embracing you. The Angel now becomes familiar to you, and you realize that this is your Guardian Angel, the same Angel that has been with you all of your life.

You begin to feel deep within you what your gifts are. It is as if they flow to the surface quickly with such grace and comfort. You know your gifts and talents.

Your Angel will show you your gifts and talents through your thoughts, insights and signs. Your Angel will show you how your gifts and talents can now be used in your life, and you become open and ready to receive. Trust and welcome the gentle, loving guidance from the Divine.

As you rest in this miracle moment and absorb all the beauty it offers, you start to become aware of your breathing again. Bring yourself back to the here and now. Slowly allow yourself to be fully present.

When you are ready, journal your experience!

Journal Prompt:

Review each of the twelve principles and how they work together in your life now within your

Goddess You Journal.

"Nancy Drew It" all the details.

The Intuitive, Gifted You

The only real valuable thing is intuition. ~Albert Einstein

By using the twelve principles, you have really opened the channels necessary to access your Inner Goddess. With all the tools you have in your belt, you are sure to rock that amazing Goddess each and every day! And if you happen to fall off your path, you can pick yourself up, dust off the old and welcome in the new groove once again. You have everything you need to rock out each day with purpose and love.

In earlier homework assignments, you spent each week focusing and setting your intent on forming a strong connection to your Inner Goddess, also known as your intuitive self. You have learned to hear her tone and feel her love and guidance. Now it is time to carry what you have learned forward into your next chapter of grooving in the world with your gifts shining.

"The intuitive mind is a sacred gift and the rational mind is a fateful servant. We have created a society that honors the servant and has forgotten the gift."
~Albert Einstein

Gifts are unique to every person. You have been graced with talents that are specific to you. How you choose to use your gifts is up to you. One of the most important things you should understand about yourself is that you have free will over your life, which is really to say you have the choice to use your gifts or not. Of course, ego has helped you to push your gifts away, keeping your thoughts in the fear pattern. Luckily, you have learned to recognize those patterns now. So, you can change your ego thought patterns to love thought patterns. It is within the love thought pattern you see, I mean really see, and know who you are, and with which gifts you have been blessed. This, my friend, is your true Goddess self rising to your own occasion!

When you discover yours, you can rock your Inner Goddess's gifts, and better understand yourself and others.

Getting to Know You

Your work is to discover your world and then with all your heart give yourself to it. ~Buddha

Knowing your main archetypes can help awaken you to your gifts. Archetypes are a way of describing universal patterns of behavior that motivate you—like the goddess, the healer or the mystic. At archetypes.com, you will find an online quiz that can help you determine your archetype. I also highly recommend the book Archetypes: **Who Are You?** by Caroline Myss, who also offers archetype resources on her website at myss. com that can help you further connect with your archetype.

Understanding Yourself on a Spiritual Level

There are so many ways to really get to know who you are, what your gifts are and what your life purpose is. The key to finding and grooving your Inner Goddess is knowing yourself on a deep, soul level. Opening without hesitation to the Divine. Believing that you are here for a purpose. Knowing that your gifts are meant to be used and that others need them. Realizing that your love is meant to flow freely without hesitation. These are the keys to finding and rocking your Inner Goddess and knowing yourself on a deep, soul level.

Forgiveness sets you free from the chains that hold you back. Remember, it is important to live forward instead of backward. It is imperative that you trust your insights and intuition. Hear what your body needs to be healthy—that's another crucial part in uncovering your Inner Goddess. This is the groove you want to live in! This is the sweet spot of knowing your Inner Goddess is one with you.

Journaling helps to reveal your true self without restrictions. Have faith in your beautiful inner voice and allow it to flow freely without judgment.

$\mathscr{H}omework$

Rehashing the past wouldn't change anything. Time to move forward. ~Zena Wynn

Now that you have discovered your gifts, it is time to connect and enhance them. One way this can be done is through meditation.

You may be wondering how exactly you can meditate on a gift. Let me share with you how Spirit has taught me to do this.

Be sure to have your journal close by so you can write down all of your impressions. The more you do this meditation, the clearer you will become on your gifts and their energy.

Gift Meditation

I start by setting the intent with Spirit to work on the gift which I have chosen to focus my effort on. I do it in the form of a prayer, which might look like this:

Dear God,

Thank you for the blessings of this gift. Please guide me with your love and the support of your Angels in using this gift of _ _ _ _ _ _ to connect to your Divine love and guidance. This guidance will bring me insight and help me or guide others who have been led to me. I have faith in your love and guidance and trust if it is your will for me to use this gift.

Amen

After I set the intention, I focus my view on the gift through the top of the head, or crown. Beautiful white or golden light opens the connection to Spirit. I stay in the connection by breathing in the energy while focusing on the breath flow. I am then led to the gift's energetic tone.

This tone can have color, shape and a feeling. Once the energy of the gift is in view, I stay within it. I ask the Angels to deepen or heal the connection. This is when they show me how the gift can grow, be used or get healed, or how to keep it at a healthy vibrational rate.

Journal Prompt:

Journal your experience

and the guidance from Spirit.

Navigating through the debris of your lifetime stories can be painful and lonely. Yet with the guidance Spirit offered you through the twelve Goddess You principles, you are now comforted and supported by the most loving Divine energy. Thus a new way of thinking and being embraces your loneliness and heals your pain. These principles have given you a spiritual support system that will continue to aid you while you embrace the shifts necessary for you to live in alignment with your Goddess Soul Self.

Yahoo!

Action Steps

- Journaling
- Meditation
- Trusting your signs
- Using your toolbox
- Living forward
- Counting blessings

You have made it through all twelve of the Goddess You principles, and I am sure you have found that they are simple yet profoundly effective. The best part is that you can return to the principles each and every day. You can go through them in any order that you like or choose one to focus on for a deeper connection. Try choosing a principle of the day and observe how it shifts your day and how it can also be used to help another. Remember to continue journaling as you move forward in this lovely Goddess soul alignment you are in.

To write was the message. Avoidance was my first reaction.

Spirit taught me that those born with the gift of being a healer are lighthouses for others who have lost their way.

Journal Prompt:

What is your message?

Are you avoiding your destiny?

The Lighthouse

The God-light that lives within each and every one of us can emerge from the fog. Faith, intention and love lead the way to the light.

Knowing you are being called to be a healer and a lighthouse requires commitment and dedication to the calling.

Following the twelve Goddess You principles, to align with your Soul Self will lead you to become a strong, bright, unwavering lighthouse of God's love.

Lighthouse Meditation

Sit with your spine straight. Set your intention to connect with God and open to your gift of being a lighthouse.

Begin with bringing your breath in through your nose, exhaling through your mouth. Allow your belly to rise fully with slow, steady breaths. Notice the breath as it fills your body. Notice how it nourishes every organ.

With each inhalation, bring the breath deeper. Allow the breath to sit in the seat of your root chakra, connecting you to your life. With each exhalation feel the release of negative stuck energy that no longer serves you.

With your intention now moving to the crown of your head, envision your crown opening fully to the Divine. The energy flow is bright, light and loving. As the energy of the Divine merges with the energy in your body, the flow of your breath will shift and clear out stored energy.

- ❀ Now with each inhale, you become lighter.

- ❀ With every exhale, you are freeing blocked energy.

- ❀ As you stay within this flow of high vibrational energy, you will feel your body shifting, muscles releasing, chakras opening.

- ❀ Merge with God as you begin to chant, "I am."

- ❀ Repeat the "I am" chant several times slowly and with intent to open fully to God.

- ❀ Shift your chant next to "I am that I am."

- ❀ Repeat the chant several times. Sway in this heightened vibration.

- ❀ Now sit quietly, open with the Divine. Your senses are alive, open and receiving.

When you are ready, slowly open your eyes and journal about your experience.

Note: This meditation opens those who are clear channels of God's love. We are all channels, although there are those who are here to aid others in healing. Be patient with your opening. There is a reason it takes time and practice. God bless.

A Final Blessing

I give you my blessing to reach far beyond what your thoughts or your dreams think are possible. I pray that you see your God-light in your own reflection so you can mirror that out to the world. I ask that the Angels be your constant guide keeping you in alignment with the Divine and your Goddess Soul Self.

Blessings and peace my friend

xx Jeanne

Acknowledgments

The process of writing The Goddess You came in many stages. Without the support of my angelic team, both heavenly and earthly, navigating my way through the process would have been impossible.

My Earth Angel Crew

To my loving parents, Pamela and Richard, who raised me with discipline, faith, love and morals. Thank you both. I love you dearly!

To Brian, my supportive, loving, understanding husband. Because you believe not only in me but also in my work, you give me the inspirational push to work, write and follow the guidance of Spirit. I love you, Street 26/26!

To Kari, my identical cousin, for the countless hours of phone calls, work days and friendship you have freely given. Your intuitive gifts and beautiful talents are how the Goddess You principles came to life. I love you, Kari Marie!

To my sister in law Eileen for lending your amazing talents and assistance as we navigated through the design and layout phase of the book. I honor and appreciate you! Love you Eileen xo!

To Colleen my friend and memory keeper, for your unwavering strength and editorial support. As always Col, you went above and beyond the call of duty. I love, honor and respect you even if I can't fully remember.

To my children and their spouses, who are my children, too: my daughter, Lauren, and her husband, Jeff; my son, Jason, and his wife, Kara; my son, Casey; and my daughter, Molly. Thank you, my loves, for your support and understanding even when you did not fully understand or know what the heck I was doing. Love you 26/26!

To my sweet grand-babies, Riley, Maisy and Hadley, I cherish every moment of being with you. My cup runneth over with a heart filled with joyful love for each of you! Love you 26/26, Mum Mum!

To my fellow light workers, whose loving support and guidance and Reiki sisterhood will be forever cherished: Pam Picard, Ellie Kukk, Kim Schmus, Carly Hilliard and Dale Barton. Love you, talented ladies!

To Marianne Williamson, whose book A Return to Love taught me how to be in God's light once again. To other writers who have illuminated my way: Gabrielle Bernstein, Eckhart Tolle, Deepak Chopra, Kris Carr, Rebecca Rosen and Doreen Virtue. You each lead with grace to teach others how to live fully in their own light. Thank you!

With a grateful heart,

Jeanne

About the Author

Author, Jeanne Street is a dynamic woman. To list her many contributions and accomplishments would be an insult to her humble nature.

Wherever there is a need, Street finds a way to lend a helping hand. Her life embodies the essence of service, compassion, gratitude and love.

She is a family first kind of woman. Devoted to her husband and soul mate of 31 years, together they are the proud parents of four grown children and grandparents to 3 and counting.

If you are lucky enough to find yourself in her inner circle, which grows daily, you will find yourself

enriched by her love and generosity. But Street does not stop with close friends and family. Her gifts are many and she longs to help as many souls as possible.

Street is a gifted spiritual medium and healer. Admittedly she has always known of these gifts, although she had not fully understood and embraced them until recent years. As she began to trust spirit's messages, they became a clear truth that she could no longer keep within.

Through her classes and client healing sessions Street is now able to witness the profound manifestation of energy shift and divine connection that her clients display. That was the catalyst for writing this book, because "when Spirit speaks, Street listens."

It has always been her deepest desire to guide others to heal themselves. Street is honored to share what has been gifted to her through her connection with Spirit in her book, *The Goddess You* principles for living In soul alignment as well as the books companion The Goddess You Journal.

You can now find Jeanne Street leading her classes and providing her healing work at her Inspirit Healing Studio at 346 Main Street, Woodbury, CT

LET'S CONNECT

This book is just the beginning of a larger conversation. I would love it if you would visit me on the web or reach out on social media.

Start at **www.jeannestreet.com** or find me on social media.

Email   jeanne@jeannestreet.com
Face Book   www.facebook.com/JeanneStreetReikiMaster
Twitter   @jeannehealer
Instagram   www.instagram.com/jeannestreetmedium
Pinterest   www.pinterest.com/jeannestreet
YouTube   www.youtube.com/channel/jeannestreet

www.inspirithealingstudio.com

Don't go it alone

Your Goddess truths are in the pages of this unique journal. Your journey begins the moment you decide to live inspired by your truths, that you are
The Goddess You!

The Goddess You
Principles for Living in Soul Alignment

Intuitive Journal

By
Jeanne Street

Illustrated by Kari Del Vecchio

You can do this! Your Goddess soul self is counting on it.

Like What you see, in
THE GODDESS YOU Series . . .

Wishing you....
Joy & Peace

Therapeutic healing modalities that will expand new opportunities for your well-being.

Navigate through your moment of need with Inspirit's qualified God based healers.

Relax your mind body and soul with one of our restorative sessions.

Master a new skill, or enhance your life with one of our diverse offerings.

Workshops ❀ Lectures ❀ Classes ❀ Private Sessions

www.inspirithealingstudio.com

CPSIA information can be obtained
at www.ICGtesting.com
Printed in the USA
BVOW05*1034211216

471206BV00002B/2/P